Coping with Russia

Coping with Russia

A Beginner's Guide to the USSR

Robert Daglish

Basil Blackwell

First published 1985
Reprinted and first published in paperback 1987

Basil Blackwell Ltd
108 Cowley Road, Oxford OX4 1JF, UK

Basil Blackwell Inc.
432 Park Avenue South, Suite 1503,
New York, NY 10016, USA

British Library Cataloguing in Publication Data
Daglish, Robert
    Coping with Russia: a beginner's guide
    to the USSR.
    1. Soviet Union
    I. Title
    947.085′4   DK17

    ISBN 0−631−13555−3
    ISBN 0−631−15441−8 Pbk

Library of Congress Cataloging in Publication Data
Daglish, Robert.
    Coping with Russia.

    Includes index.
    1. Soviet Union − Description and travel − 1970−
Guide-books.   I. Title.
DK16.D33 1985   914.7′04854   85−3962

    ISBN 0−631−13555−3
    ISBN 0−631−15441−8 (pbk.)

Typeset by Cambrian Typesetters, Frimley, Surrey
Printed in Great Britain by Billing & Sons Ltd., Worcester

Contents

For Innochka

Introduction

More people travel to Russia from the West than one might think. Britain and the United States have large embassies in Moscow. Reuters, the BBC and most of the big dailies keep permanent correspondents there. About twenty British firms, including three of the big four British banks, have their representatives in the city, and other cities where they do business. Russian and British travel agencies between them cater for almost 60,000 tourists from Britain each year. Western and Soviet universities exchange students. All kinds of Americans visit the Soviet Union in surprisingly large numbers. To take one example, the 1984 delegation of the US National Council of Churches comprised 266 US churchmen of nearly every denomination. The fact is that, despite the vagaries of the political climate, the inter-traffic has gradually increased over the past twenty years.

This is not a book about Russia's tourist attractions, about the unusual things, beautiful or ugly, one may see there. Nor do I wish to explain away the aura of mystery that surrounds Russia. For me that is part of its charm. I have often found Russian reticences as fascinating as Russian effusions. In the belief that travel to a country as huge, important and potentially rich as the USSR should and will increase, I have tried to write about what Russia is for beginners, the situations they may be confronted with and may wish to avoid, the short cuts they may not know. To some extent then the book is also about modern Russians, their ways and customs.

I hesitated to begin writing on these lines for fear of appearing trivial. A few years ago I would have said that Russia was a country for enthusiasts, people so keen to study, say, Russian ballet or archaeology, to visit some remote part of the Caucasus or Siberia, to be with some particular Russian friend or colleague, that they would make light of the difficulties and expense involved. But times are changing. The Soviet Union is becoming more and more accessible, and comfortable, for people from abroad. We do not all have to be dedicated enthusiasts to enjoy what Russia has to offer and, even if we are, we can avoid some frustrations by knowing the ropes.

A musician friend of mine who had met and liked some Russian musicians in London suddenly decided to pay them a surprise visit on New Year's Eve. He and his wife took off from Heathrow with seats already booked for a performance of *Boris Godunov* at the Bolshoi that evening. What my friend did not realise was that as many Russians as could manage it would be returning to their native land for the great occasion, the coming of the new year. There was accordingly a long and slow queue at the customs desk. By the time the two music-lovers got through it, the tickets for the opera were useless. They decided to compensate with a jolly party at a restaurant. But all the restaurants were full and, as midnight approached, the streets grew as empty as they were cold. There was nothing for it but to go back to the hotel room and hope that their friends could be contacted the next day.

Such things can easily happen to the casual visitor, artist or businessman, particularly at holiday time. The Russians celebrate eight public holidays and few if any of them coincide with those in the West.

Another difficulty I experienced in starting on this book was that it is rather a long time since I was a beginner in Russia. There are so many small everyday things I make automatic allowance for. I am not a very methodical person but at last I have learnt that most food shops in Moscow are closed from 1 p.m. to 2 p.m. for lunch, while hardware, clothes and stationery stores, etc., shut from 2 p.m. to 3 p.m. I know of a filling station near my home where I can buy petrol for cash instead of having to pay for it in vouchers bought in advance at a hardware shop or tobacconist's kiosk. These and a dozen other intricacies of Russian life are so familiar to me that it's hard to imagine anyone not knowing them. On the other hand the people who come and see me in Moscow during their first trip often spend much of the time talking about such things when we really ought to be enlightening each other with flashes of sociological insight. So why not try to get it all down on paper?

And finally, this book could not have been written without the help and advice of friends in the Soviet Union and the UK. If I have not always acted upon their advice I hope they will not take offence and will see in my approach only a sincere desire to stimulate the interflow of people and ideas.

Acknowledgements

Among the many people who helped me with this book my special thanks are due to Mr Leonard Stoklitsky who read the typescript and made invaluable suggestions.

The author and publisher would like to thank the following institutions and agencies for permission to reproduce the cartoons and maps that appear in this book. Cartoons from the magazine *Soviet Union* (VAAP) are by V. Kazanevsky (frontispiece), B. Ehrenburg (p. 30), K. Akhmerov (p. 83), Y. Rumyantsev (p. 129) and V. Tamayev (p. 133). The cartoon on p. 25 is a drawing by Modell, © 1964 The New Yorker Magazine, Inc. All other cartoons, specially commissioned for this volume, are by Vladimir Tilman and are reproduced by kind permission of VAAP. The maps were drawn for this volume. That on p. 179 is based on a map produced by the Overseas Trade Division of the Department of Trade, London; that on p. 178 is based on an Intourist map; and that on p. 180 is derived from the official map of the Moscow Metro.

Before you Start

There are more opportunities for travel to the USSR than there used to be, but you can't just show your passport, cross the border and start looking for a hotel or bed and breakfast. You must get a visa before starting out. Basically, there are two kinds of visa, *transit* and *entry/exit*. The latter may be diplomatic, tourist or ordinary. *Ordinary* visas are issued to people travelling on business or visiting relatives or friends in the USSR.

The Soviet organisation that caters for foreign travellers is known as Intourist and the address of its UK subsidiary is Intourist Moscow Ltd, 292 Regent Street, London W1R 7PO (tel. 01 631 1252/9). There is also a Manchester office. Intourist USSR has agreements with about thirty British travel agencies, who handle bookings with Moscow direct. In fact, nowadays almost every ABTA travel agent has access to Intourist services. Visitors from the US should contact Intourist at the Rockefeller Center, Fifth Avenue, Suite 868, New York, NY 10111. If you are a busy person, it is well worth paying the small fee Intourist charges for obtaining your visa for you. A visit to the Soviet consulate will probably cost you as much in fares and time. But if you are going to the USSR on the invitation of friends or relatives, you have to apply to the consulate *in person* (though arrangements in the USA are slightly different — see below).

The address of the consulate is 5 Kensington Palace Gardens, London, W8 (tel. 01-229 3215/6). They are open to visitors between 10 a.m. and 12.30 p.m., Monday to Friday, and closed at week-ends and on their public holidays, which fall on 1 January, 8 March, 1, 2 and 9 May, 7 October, and 7 and 8 November. The latest word is that they are also closed all day on Wednesdays.

To obtain a visa of any kind you will need the following:

> Three passport-size (4 X 4.5 cm) photographs, which you sign on the front along the left-hand edge (photocopies of photos are not accepted);
> A full 5- or 10-year British passport, which will still be valid a month after your date of return home;
> A completed and signed visa application form. You get this form from Intourist or from any of the British travel agencies that have agreements with Intourist when you have made your booking. It asks no questions about political affiliations.

If you have children that you are taking with you, their names can be entered on your application form unless they are over sixteen and travelling on their own passport. No photographs are required for children under seven.

When booking a tour you pay a deposit. In the unlikely event of your being refused a visa, you get your deposit back.

In addition to the above documents, to obtain a visa for a *business* trip you will have to present a letter from your company outlining your business, and a written invitation (letter, telex or cable) from the Soviet organisation you propose to have dealings with.

If you are visiting relatives or friends you will have to show a written invitation with an undertaking to provide accommodation and to cover expenses in the Soviet Union during your trip.

For a *tourist* visa you have to enclose with

your application a letter from Intourist saying you have made some kind of booking (another good reason for getting Intourist to get your visa for you).

In the United States arrangements may be a little simpler. You or your travel agent can conduct the whole operation by mail. Xeroxed copies of the relevant pages in your passport can be sent with your visa application. There are two Soviet consulates, one in Washington and the other in San Francisco (see 'Useful Addresses').

For a *transit* visa you will need a ticket valid for the continuation of your journey and a letter from Intourist confirming the arrangements for your itinerary across the country. A transit visa is valid for up to 48 hours, but if you intend stopping over for more than one day you should apply for a tourist visa.

transit visas

When travelling across Russia by air (e.g. to Japan or Sri Lanka), you do *not* need a transit visa if you will not be leaving the airport and your ticket bears a clearly stated time of departure not later than 24 hours after your arrival at the airport.

If you are travelling overland to the Soviet Union you will also need *transit* visas for any of the Eastern bloc countries you pass through on the way, and these can usually only be obtained when you have your Soviet entry visa (see above).

Any application for a visa should be made at least fourteen days before you wish to travel, but don't send it in more than six weeks beforehand.

The Russians don't charge you anything for your visa. It is a separate slip of paper. You show it on entering and hand it in on leaving the country. No stamps or other entries are made in your passport. People staying in the USSR for some time are given a residence permit, which they also hand in on leaving.

Since the Helsinki agreement, newspaper correspondents permanently accredited in the USSR have been entitled to hold multiple-use exit/re-entry visas, which enable them to travel in and out of the country without applying for a new visa each time. They do not have residence permits, but their passports are stamped.

packages If you simply want to have a holiday, enjoy the novelties and get an impression of the people, you should try one of the relatively cheap package tours offered by the travel agencies. In recent years their range has increased to take in the Baltic republics, the ancient cities of Central Asia, Black Sea holiday resorts, some parts of Siberia and a lot of other places that used not to be on the tourist map. There are also facilities for such activities as cross-country skiing, wildlife photo safaris, and shooting and fishing trips. Special tours are available for people who want to attend the various art festivals and musical competitions.

To illustrate the point about cost. The price of a one-way air ticket from London to Moscow is about £350, while an eight-day trip, including the return air fare and taking in Moscow, Suzdal and Leningrad with three meals a day, first-class hotel accommodation, skiing and sight-seeing facilities costs only £290.

Before deciding on which kind of tour to take, you should compare what Intourist has to offer with the holidays organised by a firm such as Thomson's. You may find that one or the other provides more of what you want at a lower cost.

individual travel Individual packages are also available. With these you don't travel in a group and thus have a wider choice of departure date. They cost more than group packages but not so much as going it entirely alone. Paying for your hotel room by the day is expensive because rooms for foreigners are graded first-class or de luxe and priced accordingly.

Business people can save money and time by booking only hotel accommodation and eating at the hotel restaurant as and when they need to, instead of paying for the full board that goes with a package. But in all cases book your hotel room. If you want to stay at a specific hotel, say so in advance to your travel agent.

flying to the USSR

The main air 'gateways' to the USSR from the West are London, Paris, Frankfurt, Helsinki and Vienna. From the East, Tokyo and Singapore are the most important. There are services to and from all these places operated by the Soviet airline Aeroflot and the national airlines of the countries concerned. If you come from afar (say, the United States) it is usual to change planes in Europe. But the journey will probably be cheaper if you book the whole thing from your starting point. Individual air tickets tend to be expensive, but if for some reason group travel is inconvenient, it is worth looking round for a 'bucketshop' ticket. People have been known to fly from the UK to Moscow and back for as little as £100 on such tickets. Some firms, such as Barry Martin, which have offices in New York and London, can combine the transatlantic flight with a reasonably priced ticket on to Moscow.

going by boat or train

If you intend to stay in Russia for more than a holiday, you will probably find it best to travel by rail because you can take more luggage. You can carry even more by boat, but the voyage takes five or six days, from London (Tilbury) to Leningrad, and at present there are only four sailings a year. You also have to arrange your journey from Leningrad to the capital, if that is your destination.

You might also be able to get on a boat going to Helsinki. Container ships on this run take a few passengers and cars, but the total cost would be much more than that of taking the Soviet ship, which is reasonably inexpensive, particularly the charge for the car.

The Baltic route is operated by a Soviet company known as the Baltic Steamship Company. Its agents in Britain are CTC lines, 1–3 Lower Regent Street, London SW1 (tel. 01 930 5833).

You can also reach Russia via the Mediterranean and the Black Sea (to Odessa, Yalta and Sochi), and in the Far East, you can travel from such places as Yokohama and Hong Kong to the Soviet port of Nakhodka.

the train journey There are two rail routes to Moscow from London. One is through Harwich and the Hook of Holland, and starts from Liverpool Street Station. The other is through Folkestone/Dover and Ostend and starts from Victoria Station. The journey via Holland is slightly shorter (58–60 hours) but involves a five-hour sea crossing.

The coaches for the continental part of the journey are through-sleepers. The Russians jack up your coach at the border and put wider bogies under it for their wider rail gauge. The coach compartments have three berths, one above the other. If you travel first class, only two are used and you have much more room for luggage — five or six good-sized bags.

When the train is not crowded, you may have the compartment to yourself but don't count on it. The busiest time is September, when students from all over converge on Moscow.

There is a restaurant car for most of the journey, but it's a good idea to take some

snacks and for a few pence the train steward
will keep you supplied with glasses of tea and
biscuits. Tea-bags and instant coffee or coffee-
bags are good things to take with you because
boiling water is usually available even when
hotel buffets are closed. Ask for *kipyatok*.

Make sure you have your passport and visas
in a handy place before turning in for the night.
You get woken up by East and West German
officials as the train passes through the various
sectors of Berlin. And just when you thought
it was all over, the train arrives at the Polish
border.

You can buy rail tickets to Moscow at Victoria
station in London or ask your travel agent to
obtain them. There are no boat trains, so your
booking for the two-day journey has to be
confirmed by the continental rail services.
This takes a day or two and can be inconvenient if you are not staying in London. For the
Dutch route you may be able to avoid this
bother by asking your travel agent to phone
through to Utrecht (tel. 30 353 453; the code if
calling from the UK is 010 31).

A point to remember is that you will need
East German and Polish transit visas. The
Germans will not give you a transit visa unless
they can see your Polish and Soviet visas and the
Poles will also want to be sure that you can get
into the USSR before they give you a visa to
cross their country. So take care to get the visas
in the right sequence.

visiting friends

Russians can and do invite friends from the
socialist countries to stay with them, but an
invitation to someone from the capitalist world
is a complicated business and may take months
to come through, if it comes through at all.
It is probably better, if your friends live anywhere on the tourist circuit, to pick a tour that
enables you to spend some time in that particular

town, live in a hotel and meet your friends while you are there.

If you have friends or relatives working in Russia, the procedure is simpler. They can invite you by applying to the organisation they work for (embassy or firm), which forwards the application to the appropriate Soviet authority. They then send you an invitation with an undertaking to look after you during your stay. You take this invitation to the Soviet consulate in London along with a visa application, passport etc., and when approval comes through you get your visa. Don't forget you have to collect it from the consulate *in person*.

If you are invited as a friend or colleague by organisations like the Writers' Union or the Actors' Union the Soviet consul will have received instructions to provide you with the appropriate visa on presentation of your invitation.

customs   Apart from clothes (see *Climate and Clothing*) you will obviously want to have with you various articles of personal use. Such things as cameras, electric razors and small quantities of alcohol or scent can be imported duty-free. But for more expensive items (tape recorders, video equipment and so on) you will have to certify that you intend to take them out of the country on leaving or pay a rather heavy duty. The same applies to your car, and also to personal valuables, rings, expensive watches and so on. You declare these on entry and will then be given a certificate stating how many rings, necklaces etc., you have imported.

This certificate enables you to take your valuables out of the country again. If, for instance, you are the wife of a correspondent working in Moscow and decide to make a short trip to Helsinki wearing only one ring, you should show your certificate at the customs but don't surrender it. Ask the customs man to endorse it accordingly. Surrender the certificate only when finally leaving the country with all your valuables.

The customs declaration form you complete at the border asks if you have with you any articles for third persons, i.e., something you have been asked to pass on. Officially this is not approved, so don't embarrass the customs officer by telling him one of your extra sweaters is for your friend's girl-friend in Irkutsk.

presents

The best items to bring in as gifts are souvenirs and novelties. Russians, young and old, are fond of toys. Books and records will also be appreciated, but anything considered to be anti-Soviet or pornographic may be stopped. *Playboy* magazine is an example of what the Russians regard as porn.

A point in the Helsinki agreement gives newspapermen the right to import literature connected with their work and this has been cited successfully in some cases when books have been stopped at the border.

electricity

The mains supply in Russia is at 220 volts, although a few remaining areas of 127 volts may still be found. Plugs have two round pins 2 cm apart. Electric bulbs screw into their sockets. British and Soviet radio and recording equipment are compatible but TV and video are not. Some American equipment (Realistic, for example) is wired the opposite way round and single-pin inputs need to be adjusted (in Moscow, call 276 47 14).

maps and directories

If you are a person who is never happy unless you know which point of the compass you are facing, you will want maps of the places you intend to visit. Some not very detailed maps (sightseeing or transport) are available at hotel bookstalls in the larger cities, but you can't count on getting exactly want you want, especially if it has to be in English. Collets bookshop in Charing Cross Road, London, carries a selection of maps and can help you with further inquiries.

There is a useful Moscow directory in English called *Information Moscow* (also available from Collet's, and Brentano's in New York — see also *US Information Moscow* in 'Useful Addresses'). It contains the phone numbers of Soviet governmental, trade and press institutions, service establishments, and places of entertainment, and the office and home numbers of the whole diplomatic and press corps, and the business community in Moscow.

The short telephone directory published in Moscow gives the numbers of institutions, theatres, service establishments, and so on, but to trace a personal number you have to phone directory inquiries (09) or ask at the service bureau (see p. 47).

health You don't need any health certificates if you are travelling from the UK, the United States or the Irish Republic. International smallpox vaccination certificates are required of all persons arriving from Asia, South America or Africa. Travellers from some Asian countries need a cholera vaccination certificate.

There are no special health risks about travelling in Russia apart from the cold (see p. 23), but if you expect to be in wooded country in summer, you should take with you one of the latest ointments or gadgets against mosquitoes. The Russian mosquito does not carry malaria but can be very troublesome.

insurance Under the umbrella agreement between Britain and the USSR the Russians will treat you free of charge should you fall ill or have an accident.

Hospitalisation in an emergency is also free. But there are cases when some incapacity may force you to break off your tour and incur additional expenses, for hotel accommodation, a friend to stay with you, and so on. Travel agents therefore encourage you to take out insurance providing for such eventualities. A typical policy offered by Black Sea and Baltic General Insurance gives coverage of up to £1,250 for such things as medical and travel expenses, and (God forbid, as the Russians still say) bringing home remains. I am told that if you fall off a mountain in the Caucasus or wherever, the cost of picking up the pieces and sending them home may be much more, but cases where exceptional risk is involved can also be covered. Alternatively you can resign yourself to the possibility of lying in some corner of a foreign field if your foot slips.

helpful organisations

There are several societies that could be useful to you if you are thinking of going to Russia. In the UK, the oldest of these, the Society for Cultural Relations with the USSR, founded in 1924, is run by a team of enthusiastic young people from their headquarters at 320 Brixton Road, London, SW9. They have one of Britain's best libraries of Soviet books, periodicals and slides, organise language studies and specialised tours (theatre, literature, etc.) and answer questions on anything remotely concerned with culture. Most of their staff speak Russian, have travelled in Russia and know people there.

While the SCR avoids politics, the British–Soviet Friendship Society is rather political in its aims, as its name suggests. It sprang from the many Aid-Russia committees that were set up during the war, has strong links with the trade unions and their counterparts in Russia and organises trips on this basis.

The Great Britain–USSR Association is of more recent vintage, receives a government grant, and has an imposing headquarters in Grosvenor Place. It probably has fewer contacts in Russia than the other two societies but its Establishment image is more impressive.

For people going to the USSR on business, there are many organisations in the West that can supply advice and market information. To mention only two, in the UK there are the East European Trade Council (25 Victoria Street, London, SW1) and the British–Soviet Chamber of Commerce (2 Lowndes Street, London, SW1).

checking up   A useful thing to remember before you start, and particularly before starting anything in Russia, is that no one minds you calling more than once to check up, provided you do it in time.

So check up on all departure times. The crew of your boat may have decided (collectively, of course) that if they pile on a few extra knots on the way home they can leave later and spend a few more hours in London. And you don't want to wait on the quayside while they enjoy themselves.

Money

The ordinary Soviet rouble in circulation in the obtaining roubles USSR is not convertible and cannot be taken in or out of the country. So don't bother asking your bank to get roubles for you. Since you can't take roubles into the USSR, you buy them for cash or traveller's cheques on arrival. At the border you will be asked to declare all the hard currency and traveller's cheques you have with you. You do this by entering the amounts on a form, which is then endorsed by a customs officer and handed back to you. At the exchange bureau you change as much as you think you will need into roubles and get a receipt. Keep the form and the receipt throughout your stay, so that you can convert any unspent roubles back into hard currency when you leave. Otherwise you will have to leave them behind in a savings bank.

There are exchange facilities at border-crossing points (e.g., airports) and at hotels that cater for foreigners. You are advised to use the airport facility if arriving late at night, as the hotel bureaux will probably be closed. There is no *bureau de change* at Universitetskaya, the hotel where visiting scholars usually stay. But don't change all your hard currency. You should keep some by you for shopping at the Beryozka hard-currency shops, which sell souvenirs, cameras, fur hats and the like, and sometimes food, drink and clothes (see the chapter on Shopping and Services).

You can use any of the well-known traveller's traveller's cheques and credit cards cheques all along the main tourist routes in Intourist hotels, restaurants and at hard-currency

(Beryozka) shops. If you have only cash with you and don't want to carry it about, you can buy Soviet traveller's cheques on arrival. In Moscow this can be done at the Foreign Trade Bank in the International Trade Centre. The commission is ½%.

The credit card system is also fairly well established at hotels along the main tourist routes. In 53 cities you can use American Express, Visa, Diners Club (Eurocard), Access, MasterCard and Carte Blanche. The advantage of the credit card over the traveller's cheque is that you can pay your bill exactly without having to wait for the person at the cash desk or the waiter in a restaurant to find the change in the currency you want, but it is less expensive to use traveller's cheques for purchasing the roubles you will need in ordinary shops, restaurants, on public transport etc. In the USSR Eurocheques have to be made out in US dollars and can be cashed only at the Bank for Foreign Trade or the State Bank.

roubles and kopecks   Rouble notes come in denominations of 1, 3, 5, 10, 25, 50, and 100. There is also a one-rouble silver-coloured coin.

The rouble is worth 100 kopecks. Kopecks are always coins. The 10, 15, 20 and 50 kopeck pieces are silver in colour, but the 1, 2, 3 and 5 kopeck pieces are copper. One kopeck is a tiny coin but not to be sneezed at. Two of them pay for a local phone call and for five you can travel from one side of Moscow to the other by bus or underground (Metro). But other less basic items are by no means as cheap, and for these you pay far less in hard currency at the duty-free Beryozka shops.

It's *illegal* to buy roubles anywhere except at the official exchange bureaux or to sell clothing or other belongings to Soviet citizens. The law is rather vigilant on this point and it's better not to be tempted, even if you only wish to do someone a favour.

If you find yourself in need of extra cash, you can arrange a transfer from your home bank through the Bank for Foreign Trade (usually abbreviated as *Vneshtorgbank*). In Moscow this is located in the International Trade Centre on the Krasnopresnenskaya Embankment (see the map on p. 179). English is spoken and you can contact them by phone (253 17 99). At this bank you can also open an account in sterling or any other hard currency. Amounts of over 10,000 hard-currency roubles, deposited for a fixed term of 1, 3, 6 months or a year, earn a reasonable interest.

If you are working in the USSR and being paid in roubles, you should put any money you have to spare in a Savings Bank (*sberkassa*). There are branches in every district and the procedure is very simple. You can transfer such an account to any place in the USSR, authorise other people to draw on it, or bequeath it to anyone whose name you choose to write on a form and leave with the branch.

If you are staying in another town and run out of roubles, you can telegraph your branch of the *sberkassa*. Quote the number of your bank book and ask them to telegraph some money back. Except at weekends this should not take more than two days. The postal expenses are debited to your account.

banking money in the USSR

The Feel of the Country

'Russia' and the USSR

Russia is only part of the Union of Soviet Socialist Republics and Russians account for just over half of the population. But I have used 'Russia' in the title of this book because Russia, that is to say the Russian Federal Republic, is the largest of the fifteen republics that make up the USSR, or Soviet Union, and Russians are the people you are most likely to meet if you go there. And also because with a little knowledge of the Russian language you can make yourself understood in all the other republics. In other words 'Coping with Russia' is the first step towards 'Coping with the USSR'.

The Soviet Union is vast, the largest country in the world. Its fifteen republics cover an area of 8,500,000 square miles and extend across eleven time zones. But large parts are either arctic or sub-arctic and you won't have to cope

with them, unless you happen to become a member of some professional expedition, in which case you will know more about polar exploration than I do.

Russian character

The biggest mistake you can make is to start generalising about the Russians as soon as you set foot in the country. For one thing there are so many of them and, besides, Russia is still a huge ethnic and social melting pot. But for some reason the temptation to generalise is irresistible, and it grows on you the longer you stay.

The sense of vastness colours the mentality of most Soviet people, even those who have spent all their lives in the big cities. It inspires both awe and pride. Russians are also fond of small things, of intimacy and cosiness, but these they may suddenly grow tired of and throw aside like a toy. They can be surprisingly frank and also extremely secretive. They yearn for open spaces, yet they like things that are hidden and mysterious. There is much to be said for the notion of Russia as a land of contrasts, but the scale is so vast that you must be prepared for great slabs of monotony as well.

Perhaps this accounts for the massive element of calm in the Russian character. Despite the flare-ups you may sometimes witness, Russians are not easily excited or enraged. But when finally aroused, in love or anger, the effect is apt to be lasting.

In the course of the upheavals, wars and huge development schemes of the present century most Russians have moved about the country a good deal and there has also been much intermingling of the peoples. When you get to know a Russian, or any Soviet person, at all well, you will often find that he thinks of himself as having not just one *ródina* (native land) but two — the Soviet Union as a whole and some little corner of it where he was born. And he has a

special word for a man from that particular
corner — *zemlyák*, a man of his own soil. So it's
a good thing to know how Russians divide up
their country geographically.

North   When the Russians speak of the north (*sévyer*),
they don't mean Leningrad, although Leningrad
is farther north than the north of Scotland —
indeed, farther north than much of Canada.
They have in mind places like Arkhangelsk and
Murmansk, and the great peninsulas butting into
the Arctic Ocean. Murmansk is the northern-
most point you can reach with Intourist and the
trip is practical only in spring or summer because
of the polar night. In March, when the sun
reappears over the horizon, a 'Northern Sports
Festival' is held there. At a lower latitude,
Lake Onega and the Island of Kizhi with the
midnight sun and an abundance of wild flowers
show you the gentler side of the Russian north.

South   For most Russians *yoog* (the south) is the
mountain-sheltered coast of the Crimea and the
Caucasus, where they go for holidays by the
Black Sea during the hot summer and the
'velvet' autumn. In the Caucasus and Transcau-
casus there are three republics — Georgia,
Armenia and Azerbaijan. Rather like those
Russian dolls with smaller dolls inside them,
each republic comprises smaller nationalities,
which are organised according to size into
autonomous republics, regions, and so on. In all,
the Caucasus with its snow-capped mountains
and sub-tropical coasts accommodates about
fifty nationalities.

  But there are other parts of the country that
lie further south than this and are much hotter,
such as Ashkhabad in Turkmenia, which borders
on Iran. The four republics along these southern-
most borders — Turkmenia, Uzbekistan, Tajik-
istan and Kirghizia — are known as the Central

Asian Republics. Even today they differ considerably from Russia in dress and customs. They have modern transport and mechanised agriculture, but somehow their history seems very near the surface. The city of Samarkand, in Uzbekistan, was once the capital of Timur's Mongul Empire. Legend has it that before he died, Timur said any man who disturbed his tomb would bring an invader to his country more terrible than he. The tomb was opened by archaeologists — in June 1941.

East For Soviet people, the 'Far East' (*Dálny Vostók*) is the broad coastal strip along the Pacific Ocean, facing Alaska in the far north and Japan in the sub-tropical south, and including the large offshore island of Sakhalin. Inland lies the enormous expanse of forests, mountains, lakes, rivers and marshes known as Siberia, the 'sleeping land', from a Tatar word meaning 'slumber'. It is by no means so fast asleep as it was when the name was coined, but many of its vast resources are only beginning to be tapped.

Siberia is usually divided into Western and Eastern, the former marshy and low-lying with enormous stocks of oil, the latter mountainous

and rich in minerals, gold and diamonds. The
twenty million people who inhabit this region
are mostly Russians and Ukrainians by origin,
with enclaves of indigenous peoples, Chukchi,
Evenks, Eskimos, etc., especially in the far north.
They all call themselves Siberians (*Sibiryakée*)
and speak of Russia as beginning west of the
Urals. The region is traversed by one railway,
the famous Trans-Siberian, from which branch
lines run for several hundred miles north and
south, then just stop. But the recently built
main line known as BAM, from Lake Baikal to
the River Amur, has given Eastern Siberia a
new dimension. Baikal is the world's deepest
lake and contains one-fifth of all the fresh water
on the earth's surface. The appearance of a large
paper mill on its shores in the early 1970s
roused controversy and made Russians much
more environment-conscious than in the days
when their natural resources seemed invulnerable
to even the most vigorous industrial development. They now talk almost as much as anyone
else about environmental protection.

**Central
Russia**
The Ural Mountains are the natural divide
between Europe and Asia. Viewed from this
angle, Moscow, a thousand miles to the West,
belongs almost in Western Europe and some
modern Russian writers like to recall the days
when Muscovy was the shield of Christian
Europe against the Tatars.

A gently undulating forested plain watered by
the Volga, Dnieper and a dozen smaller rivers,
this is really the heartland of Russia and you can
get a good notion of it by visiting such cities as
Novgorod, Smolensk, Yaroslavl, Suzdal, and
Kursk. With their kremlins and cathedrals, even
the most industrialised still remind you of a
more rural but not always peaceful past. In 1943
Kursk and the country round it was the scene of
the Russian victory in the crucial tank battle of

the Second World War, during which for fifty days, in fighting of unparalleled intensity, Germans and Russians killed each other at the rate of 20,000 lives a day.

There are five republics in the western part of **West** the USSR — Lithuania, Latvia and Estonia, ranged along the Baltic coast in the north-west; Byelorussia in the west, and Moldavia in the south-west. In the Baltic republics there are many signs of Germanic and Polish influence, especially in the architecture and general neat-ness of the cities and their people. Russians often think of themselves as having travelled West when they take a holiday on the Baltic, and Soviet films about Western Europe are often shot there. Solidly built private houses are much in evidence, in contrast to the large apartment blocks with many a surviving log cabin in between that you find in the suburbs of most Russian cities. Byelorussia, on the other hand, is barely distinguishable from the rest of Russia, perhaps because it has had to bear the brunt of so many invasions and rebuildings. But the language is different, and a less sweeping view than we are taking at the moment would detect many subtle differences in character and custom.

Moldavia with its mountains and vineyards is picturesque and richly agricultural, like the Ukraine on to which it backs. The Ukraine is the second of the Soviet republics in population. Here you have the rich black soil and steppe which extend across the Dniester and Dnieper river basins to the Kuban and the Don, once the steppeland abode of the Cossack cavalry armies, but now highly cultivated, with an industry that manufactures, among other things, reactors for atomic power stations.

Going east again, we cross the Volga and come to Kazakhstan, which used to be mainly virgin steppe but has undergone intensive economic development since the launching of the Virgin Lands scheme in the 1950s and is now an important grain producer, despite the fact that two out of every five harvests may be expected to fail because of the hot dry winds from the east. Its rugged steppes have also provided a starting and returning ground for the Soviet space shots.

Climate and Clothing, Natural Hazards

From the above lightning trip round the fifteen republics you will probably conclude that you have to be ready for some contrasting weather.

The USSR does have a wide range of climate but in winter, by British standards at least, most of it is cold. Siberia, of course, is the coldest, and temperatures there average between −20 and −30 °C (45° of frost F) through January and February. But the thermometer is not the only indicator of cold, and in Leningrad or the Baltic republics, where the air from the north often mingles with the damp Atlantic air stream, you may feel a lot chillier than in a hard central Russian frost.

Winter does not set in all at once, not in Moscow anyway. It attacks in rushes of cold wind and snow from the north, which are often followed by a thaw. So in November and December you have to be prepared for slushy weather, when the drains are choked with half-melted snow. Some kind of rubber overshoe or boots with thick spongy soles (moon boots are good) make the best kind of footwear. In any case, a thick sole is essential, because the cold, wet or dry, strikes through a thin one in no time.

You will need a well-lined overcoat or sheepskin, preferably fairly long, although the fashionable thing nowadays is the quilted spacesuit type of jacket or coat filled with man-made fibre (or goosedown, if you can afford it). These have the advantage of being very light and consequently less tiring, but don't forget that most Russians who sport them are wearing long johns as well under their jeans. These are great for long spells in the open, and for when you get into your car after leaving it for an hour or so in the frost, and they don't make you too hot indoors. Men who forget to bring a pair can keep their pyjama trousers on under their slacks, which is almost as good in an emergency.

Don't bundle yourself up with thick woollen vests and roll-neck sweaters. Most Russian interiors are warmly heated and you will feel uncomfortable in a sweater that you can't easily take off. Anyone accustomed to sleeping in an old-fashioned English bedroom will almost certainly find Russian hotel rooms too warm for comfort. Most of them have small ventilation panes in the double glazing, but if yours hasn't, don't try to open the whole window yourself. Ask what can be done to make the room cooler. In the absence of an interpreter, just say 'dóoshno' and look as if you can't breathe.

In the old days most Russians used to wear galoshes over ordinary walking shoes or, in the country, over felt top-boots. This was such a sensible habit that it may come back (in rural areas it hasn't been abandoned). The double layer gave ample protection and, because the galoshes were easy to slip off at the threshold, you never made your host's floors dirty. However, the coming of the fashion boot did away with all that. Some people now bring shoes with them when visiting friends. Don't imagine that a quick wipe at the door will be good enough — melting snow mixed with road sand will form a lovely puddle later on.

headgear and gloves Fur hats are fun and you will probably want to wear one, even if it feels rather hot when you are travelling by Metro. But except in very cold weather any kind of hat or woollen cap will do, as long as you can pull it down far enough to protect the upper part of your ears from frost

'Nyet'

bite. If you have sensitive ears, you should
always have ear flaps. On a winter trip bring
gloves or mittens with you as you may not be
able to find the kind you want in a local shop.
Mittens give you much better protection than
gloves. Fur hats are usually available in Beryozka
shops for hard currency, but they are rather
expensive, the cheapest currently being about
£30.

If you come from a land with a temperate
climate, you will have to get used to gauging the
temperatures. Anything below freezing-point
sounds terribly cold, but after a few weeks
you will soon find yourself talking like any
Russian about the warm weather today, when it

is only three or four below — and leave off a few layers accordingly.

Wind is an important factor. Out skiing, you can be quite warm in a snowed-up forest but chilled to the bone crossing a windswept field. A hard frost in still weather is far more pleasant than a strong south wind and a temperature hovering around freezing point. Early February, often Moscow's coldest month, is one of the best times of year because of the cold crisp air and the lengthening days.

weather forecasts

Moscow Information, the twice-weekly supplement to *Moscow News*, carries a weather forecast in English, and the Nine o'clock News on television concludes at about 9.30 p.m. with a round-up of forecasts for the main cities, spoken and visual. A detailed forecast for the whole country comes up at 8 p.m. on Moscow Radio's second programme Mayak (549 kHz), but for that you have to understand Russian.

spring

The swift Russian spring doesn't always live up to its reputation, but it's a lot more sudden than an English spring, and after the long winter one feels enlivened and enervated in turns. Russian poets still like to talk about the languors of spring but Russian doctors prescribe vitamin tablets, which are cheap and plentiful.

The weather starts getting warmer at different times in different places. The Crimean coast is warm by April and quite hot in May, although the sea will still be cold. Further south, in the Caucasus, temperatures rise sooner but you may expect more rain. Moscow and Central Russia generally lag almost a month behind the Black Sea coast, and Armenia and the Central Asian republics may be two or three weeks ahead. Moscow can be very hot in the second half of May, but snow has been known to fall on May

Day. East of the Urals, cold snaps occur even in June.

summer

Moscow and even Leningrad may have very hot summers, but the heat begins to abate rapidly in the second half of August. Kiev and the Ukraine stay warm a little longer. For comfort in summer you need really lightweight clothing, but you must also be prepared for a cold wind or two and some rain. In town an umbrella is a good thing. Often the showers are heavy but brief and the air remains sultry.

Incidentally, clocks are put forward by one hour during Summer Time in all eleven time zones. Summer Time begins on the last Sunday in March and ends on the last Sunday in September.

autumn

Around Moscow the leaves begin to turn at the end of August, and for a few weeks in September the forests are a glorious sight. Sometimes the weather suddenly grows quite warm and there is an Indian summer — the Russians call it Women's Summer (*bábye léto*). It's one of the best times of the year but, as the name implies, it does not last long and soon afterwards you are deep in autumn. In October there is often snow on the ground, but you can still walk in the woods and enjoy the cool scented air until more snow falls and you need a pair of skis.

natural hazards

The great Russian plain (actually it's quite hilly in places) does not present many natural hazards. Drought, flooding and hail do a lot of harm to crops, but these are problems for the farmer. During droughts you will have to be very careful not to start a forest fire, and traffic patrols will be even more particular than usual about your driving off the road only at lay-bys and camp sites. During the worst droughts of recent years the peat bogs round Moscow caught fire and even hikers had to keep out of the woods for fear of collapses caused by creeping combustion underground. For the motorist the main hazard is the state of the roads, which suffer badly from frost heaves and heavy truck traffic (see the chapter on driving, pp. 79 ff.).

Tornadoes are rare. About once in twenty years they do hit places in Central Russia. But these are freaks and the main feature of the Russian countryside is a peacefulness that varies only with the seasons.

wild animals There is little danger either from wild animals. The elk and deer that roam in the forest parks round Moscow are timid and you would have to get well off the beaten track to meet a wolf, bear or wild boar. But all of these are dangerous, particularly the wild boar. If you do happen to meet a wolf, you will be able to dine out on the event for weeks afterwards. But don't run

away because, then, he might dine out on you. The rule is to face up to him and edge sideways off his territory. Don't be overcome by curiosity if you spot a wild boar and his family. The male will certainly attack if you approach. In the remoter parts of the country, of course, the incidence of bears and wolves is much higher and around Lake Baikal tourists are usually warned not to venture into thickets of wild raspberries, where 'Meeshka' may also have decided to feast himself.

In wooded country mosquitoes are a real nuisance. The only consolation is that they don't carry malaria. Russians tend to put up with them stoically and laugh at the inefficiency of the repellents sold by chemists. But watch out for gadflies, especially after bathing, and swat them as soon as they settle on you. This is easy because they become quite reckless at the prospect of tasting blood. Cover the parts of you that you can't watch. The same applies in the case of ticks and mites, which occasionally swarm in the forests.

biting insects

In the mountains of the Caucasus and Central Asia there are hazards in plenty for the adventurous — falling stones, land and mud slides, avalanches, and snakes. But people who climb mountains presumably want something to nearly happen to them, apart from the possiblity of falling a few thousand feet.

Central Asia has quite a reputation for snakes, spiders and scorpions. I once spent two months in Bukhara on a film location. Before I went, my friends were at pains to warn me of the dangers I faced and how to survive them. On the way to the airport, the taxi driver had many more comforting remarks on the subject. Questioned about spiders, he took his hands off the wheel in a gesture that could only be interpreted as a death wish for me and himself.

scorpions

The only scorpion I saw was the one we eventually tracked down for a part in our picture. It proved to be almost invisible against the sand and had to have ink poured over it, after which it became even less ready to face the camera, and its part was eliminated from the script. Apparently, scorpions are only really active in the month of May, when their sting may be fatal. For the rest of the time they lurk under stones in quiet places. So be a little careful when visiting old ruins. As for snakes and spiders, they are rarely seen in town but shake

your shoes in the morning just in case. Incidentally, there is one poisonous snake, the common European viper, that is sometimes found in the forests of Central Russia. This is another good reason for wearing boots if you go into the woods.

In the Far East, of course, anything may happen. Typhoons sometimes blow in from the Sea of Japan and the Ussuri tiger can't be quite as harmless as he looks on the screen, when the trappers have done with him.

There are lakes and reservoirs everywhere and people seem to bathe in them without fear of pollution, but it is best to stick to officially recognised beaches, where a small charge is sometimes made.

If an old lady stops in her tracks and says something that sounds rather uncomplimentary as you sally past her bareheaded on a wintry morning, she might be exclaiming *shápkoo própil*, which means literally 'he's drunk his hat away' or 'he spends so much money on drink, he can't afford a hat'. There's no need to be offended. She's only thinking of the danger of your catching meningitis in a hard frost — the worst fear of all Russian mothers with headstrong sons.

dressing for the occasion

This is about the only stricture concerning dress you are likely to encounter. Russians are not half so formal about clothes as they used to be in the 1950s and 1960s. Western jeans suits, T-shirts and the like are now very much the 'in' thing, at least among the younger generation. Perhaps the only thing that surprises the native nowadays is the sight of some young Westerner in a Russian country store buying the thick padded jacket and trousers worn by outdoor workers in cold weather. That seems a bit too much like spending money on a busman's holiday. Some Russians still expect foreigners to look different from themselves and may even be a bit disappointed if they don't.

informality

The new informality has made your summer dress problem much easier. In a hot and crowded theatre or concert hall, shirt sleeves and open necks are quite in order. But such freedom does not extend to diplomatic or business receptions or interviews with famous people, for which a touch of formality will be appreciated. Full evening dress is never needed, although women's evening dress is becoming more and more elaborate. Oddly enough, in circles where women tend to dress rather plainly, slacks are frowned upon as highly informal. Russian men wear dinner jackets only for performing at concerts or on the stage.

nudism   Some resorts have special beaches where the sexes bathe and sunbathe separately in the nude. But public nudism is not accepted. It would be considered an affront for anyone to walk down a city main street stripped to the waist, even in the hottest weather. Shorts are seldom worn except at holiday resorts.

The Soviet attitude to dress is still well summed up in the old Russian saying, 'We meet you according to your dress and see you off according to your mind.' Or to put it more clearly, 'Our first impression is of your clothes but what counts with us in the long run is your brains.'

The Language—How to Get By

The difficulties of Russian have probably been exaggerated — it's just as easy to speak Russian badly as any other language. Which is what Russians will expect you to do for at least your first ten years in the country. After that they may stop praising your exceptional linguistic ability and express some surprise at the persistence of your English accent. But don't let that prospect worry you. All you need to know on a first trip is how to get by. And that is not such a problem as it may seem.

Don't be intimidated by the extra letters in the alphabet. In the long run they make pronunciation easier for you. By providing separate letters for most sounds the Russians have made it simpler to read words as they are written and arrive roughly at the correct pronunciation.

копинг
**with the
alphabet**

Admittedly, there is the tricky problem of stress and the effect that one sound may have on another in certain combinations, but I shall come to that when we have had a look at the alphabet.

Russian letter		Pronounced as
А	а	a in *after* (but when unstressed, as a in *about*)
Б	б	b in *bat*
В	в	v in *vat*
Г	г	g in *girl*
Д	д	d in *dot* (but as 't' at the end of a word)
Е	е	ye in *yes*
Ё	ё	yo in *yonder*
Ж	ж	zh like 's' in *treasure*

З	з	z in *zest*
И	и	i in *if* (but 'ee' as in *see* when stressed)
Й	й	y in *joy*
К	к	k in *keep*
Л	л	l in *lion*
М	м	m in *mother*
Н	н	n in *not*
О	о	o in *or* (but when unstressed, as 'u' in *but*)
П	п	p in *pull*
Р	р	r in *roll* (but roll it a bit more)
С	с	s in *sun*
Т	т	t in *tall*
У	у	oo in *boot* (usually transcribed as 'u')
Ф	ф	ff in *off*
Х	х	h in *hot* (usually transcribed as 'kh')
Ц	ц	ts in *cats*
Ч	ч	ch in *chat*
Ш	ш	sh in *shot*
Щ	щ	shch in *gesture*
Ъ	ъ	hard sign (separates sounds normally elided)
Ы	ы	i in *with*
Ь	ь	soft sign (softens mainly d, l, and t)
Э	э	e in *extra*
Ю	ю	yu in *yule*
Я	я	ya in *yarn*

The first thing you notice is that 'c' has apparently disappeared and that both the second and third letters of the alphabet look rather like 'b'. But what has actually happened is that 'c' has been relegated to eighteenth place in the alphabet, because in Russian it is always pronounced like 's', and its position as third letter has been given to the Russian в, which is our 'v'.

Now take a closer look at the Russian л,п,ф.

Borrowed from the Greek, they are not unlike their English equivalents l, p, and f. Just remember that л is thinner and ф fatter, and that we, too, use п, in geometry.

So once you realise that the Russian letters в, н, р, с, are not what they seem but, in fact, represent the same sounds as the English v, n, r, and s, you will have half the alphabet under control.

Of the newcomers ж represents a sound you may think we don't have till you recall such words as 'leisure', 'measure', 'treasure', etc.

Four other newcomers ц, ч, ш, щ are an easy group to remember. If you take them in descending order, they grow thicker in print, and so do their sounds *ts*, *ch*, *sh*, and *shch*. Bernard Shaw would have rejoiced over how much printer's ink and compositor's labour have been saved by using single letters for sounds that the Latin alphabet expresses only by two- and four-letter combinations.

stress

With all these advantages suddenly bestowed upon you, you will be saddened to discover that you still can't pronounce Russian correctly unless you somehow manage to get the stress right. There are no simple rules. The only way to make progress is to listen carefully when people correct you and (if you decide to learn the language) to read as many stressed texts as possible. It also helps to consider for a moment where the main stress falls in some English words. This will attune your ear to emphasis in general.

Russian is partly English and French

Once you know the alphabet, you will begin to recognise dozens of Russian words that are similar in English and other European languages. Starting from the аэропóрт (airport), you will collect your багáж (baggage), be met by a гид (guide), get into an автóбус or a таксú (bus or taxi), have a meal in a ресторáн (restaurant) or a буфéт (buffet), speak on the телефóн (telephone), go to the óпера (opera) or балéт (ballet), and so on.

You will also find, if your business is with science or technology, that large numbers of words with Latin or Greek roots are available to you almost unchanged, except for a few letters or the stress. 'Biology', for instance, is биолóгия and a 'biologist' is a биóлог. Incidentally, Russians tend to make the names for practitioners of such disciplines by cutting off the ending rather than adding a new one. Thus a 'mathematician' is a *matemátik*, and a photographer (watch out!) is a *fotógraf* (pronounced *futáwgraf*).

Of course, you can't be sure that some imported words won't have changed their meaning during their stay in Russia. '*Fábrika*', for instance, is not a 'fabric', but the place where fabric is made — a factory. And a *mashéena* is a 'machine' mainly in the sense of a car or some other means of road transport.

avoiding the verb As soon as they try to speak a foreign language, people start constructing enormously complicated polite phrases. This probably dates from their schooldays when language teachers wanted them to learn how to conjugate verbs. But this chapter is mainly about avoiding such painful operations, and you will be glad to hear that in the present tense Russians hardly ever use the verb 'to be'. They just say я фотóграф meaning 'I am a photographer' or он дóктор 'he is a doctor'. So let me consolidate this point by giving you the personal pronouns right away.

I	я	you	вы	he	он
me	меня́	you	вас	him	его́
to me	мне	to you	вам	to him	ему́
she	она́	we	мы	they	они́
her	её	us	нас	them	их
to her	ей	to us	нам	to them	им

A glance at this table will suggest to you that the plural ending in Russian is probably formed by adding an 'i'. And so it is, with a few exceptions in 'a'. The 'i' is sometimes hard, sometimes soft (but you don't need to bother about that). So we get мужчи́ны (men), же́нщины (women), де́ти (children), маши́ны (cars), and so on.

greetings

Now that you have a few of the basics, what you need is some polite phrases to help them along and to make life generally more pleasant.

You don't need to know the Russian for 'good morning' or 'good evening'. Just say *zdrástvooyetye* (literally, 'good health to you'). This is what Russians say to each other every day when they first meet, whether in the morning, afternoon or evening. Sometimes they say 'good morning' (*dóbroye útro*) as well, but that doesn't matter. The obligation to say *zdrástvooyetye* first is on the person coming into the house, office, etc., and on young people meeting their seniors. But don't use it twice to the same person on the same day or he will think you didn't notice his response, which was also *zdrástvooyetye*.

There are a dozen different ways of saying *zdrástvooyetye*, from a cheerful bellow to a formal mutter, but it will always be appreciated. It is also a nice simple response when you are being introduced.

requests

Pozhálsta (please) and *spaséebo* (thank you) also make life a lot pleasanter. In fact, *pozhálsta* is so important you should make it the main word in your vocabulary. It can be used to express all kinds of requests. Say it with a long and resonant 'ah' in the middle and only a faint ending. Suppose, for instance, you are somewhere near, but cannot find, the Metro. Just go up to someone who doesn't look in too much of a

hurry and say *pozhálsta, Metró?* And he will probably guess what you want.

  Pozhálsta is also used in the sense of 'certainly', 'go ahead', 'help yourself'. Like the Russian *da* (yes), it is often repeated a couple of times in quick succession for emphasis. The Russian *nyet* (no) is sometimes followed up with *nye nádo* (literally, 'it's not necessary'), which can mean anything, from plain 'don't' to 'better not' or 'don't bother', depending on the tone of voice. *Nádo* is often used without the *nye*. Like the French *il faut*, it's too impersonal for English, but in its native setting it punches a terse message home. Whenever you feel something is essential or inescapable, just say *nádo*. Our 'musts' and 'no ways' are the modern English equivalents.

  The well-known Russian *neechevó* means literally 'nothing', but is often used in the more positive sense of 'there's nothing wrong', 'never mind' or 'not bad'.

making your views known You will also need to express your attitude to various situations. Most Russian adjectives can be made into adverbs by substituting 'o' for the last syllable, which enables you to comment on actions as well as things. So *huróshy* (good) becomes *hurushó*, and *plukhóy* (bad) becomes *plókho*. Get the stress right and you can express 'you're doing well' or 'you've made a mess of it' in just one word.

  The 'o' form also has the sense of 'too'. If the

hairdresser has turned on the cold tap too hard while washing your hair, a prompt *hólodno!* will put her right. And it will actually be better Russian than the full form *sléeshkom hólodno!* (too cold!). Use intonation as much as possible to express your meaning and you will be well on the way to developing a Russian manner of speaking.

The Russian *nye* (not) can be put in front of **opposites** many positive words to give them opposite meaning. Sometimes it has only a moderating effect. *Nyehurushó*, for instance, means 'not fair!' or 'not nice'. But the addition of *nye* is a useful trick when you are short of words.

The absence of articles, definite or indefinite, **articles** and the Russians' sparing use of possessives will also make your task easier once you have got the knack. It may even lead you to ponder on why we always need to say 'I put *my* hand in *my* pocket', whereas a Russian merely says *ya puluzhéel róokoo v karmán* (I put hand in pocket) and assumes you will draw the right conclusions.

Whatever the reasons (and language is not always reasonable), this economical way of speaking is a boon to us because the Russians, like other continental Europeans, do have a very extravagant habit of making adjectives and nouns agree through a complicated system of case endings, which I shall not even begin to go into. Suffice it to say that any confusion that may be caused by the lack of articles or possessives can often be removed by the simple expedient of using 'this' (*eto*) or 'that' (*to*). Of course, to be correct, you have to make them agree with the thing you are talking about, but people will still understand you even if you don't.

apologies All these remarks about what you don't need to bother about in Russian should not make you think Russian is a crude or primitive language. On the contrary, the Russian verb that we have been at such pains to avoid is an amazingly flexible and subtle means of expression, and the case endings that we cannot at this stage attempt have made the language one of the most musical in Europe, comparable only to Italian for its melodious flow. So for your efforts to speak Russian in your own crude fashion, you will occasionally have to apologise, especially if your requests are fully understood and spark off a voluble response. In all cases, the word is *izvinéetye* — *izvinéetye, ya plókho guvuryú po-róosky*; *izvinéetye, ya nye punimáyu* (Sorry, I speak Russian badly; Sorry, I don't understand). And this can be followed up with *Pozhálsta, myédlenno* (Slowly, please) or *Pozhálsta, yeshchó raz* (Once again, please). And another, conveniently short apology, if you happen to bump into somebody or tread on their foot, is *veenovát* (Sorry, my fault).

However, if this attempt to encapsulate the
Russian language in a few pages has only left
you more confused than when we started, don't
imagine you are going to be utterly lost and
unable to communicate. Quite a few Russians
speak English and many more learnt some at
school but have almost forgotten it for lack of
practice. So why not give them the chance to
bring it back?

use English
instead

Some Russians speak quite good American,
or what sounds like American to an English
ear. But remember, if an American-speaking
Russian invites you to be at the theatre at 'ten
of seven', he wants you to get there at 'ten
minutes to seven'. Confusingly, however, the
Russian *désyat minóot sedmóva* (ten minutes
of seven) means *ten minutes past six*! So, to be
sure, it's probably best to stick to figures and
the twenty-four-hour clock.

Communicating

Moscow and other cities are well supplied with
public telephones — *telefón-avtomát*, or simply
avtomát. Don't be put off by the fact that a lot
of them nowadays are called *taksofón*. It has
nothing to do with taxis. It merely means that
your call is limited to three minutes, after which
you have to insert another two kopecks and dial
again. Don't just put some more money in and
hope the connection will come back.

The *avtomát* is a very simple instrument. You
lodge your 2 kopeck piece (*dvóoshka*) or two
single kopecks, in the slot at the top, dial the
number and, when somebody answers, your
money drops and you're through. Sometimes
it drops without getting you through, which is
too bad, because there is no button for coin
recovery. You just have to be well supplied with
dvóoshki, which is a very small sum anyway.
If there is one box that everybody seems to
avoid, it is probably out of order. Don't expect
it to be labelled as such or sealed off. Just don't
use it.

An advantage of the new *taksofón* is that it
will take some of the weight off the system,
which because calls are so cheap tends to be
overloaded.

If you are used to the British manner of
always announcing your number when you lift
the receiver, you may be disconcerted by the
Russian habit of just saying *ullo* (hullo) or *da*
(yes). Russians are rather cagey about disclosing
their private number, so just go straight ahead
and ask for whoever it is you want. If you find
yourself consistently getting what appears to be
the wrong number, don't ask what number it is.

Ask whether it is the number you think you have been dialling.

Funnily enough, quite a few callers break this rule. Failing to recognise your voice as the one they want (the approved method of checking the number seems to be voice recognition), they ask, 'What number is that?' And funnier still, after a while you will find yourself replying, 'What number do you want?'

It seems that Russians much prefer a bit of fencing to start with and a long, timeless conversation afterwards than to have to disclose something as private as their own telephone number to all and sundry.

don't write, phone

The telephone plays an enormous part in Soviet life and you should use it as much as possible. If you have no Russian, always ask your interpreter to make telephone inquiries for you rather than start by writing a letter. An organisation that requires a letter from you will tell you *on the phone* what kind of letter is needed. People may be quite willing to answer your inquiry, but they won't want the trouble of getting a letter typed, approved, numbered and sent, as all official letters have to be. They may well assume that sooner or later you will repeat your inquiry by phone. Of course, replies to letters from abroad are a different matter, but much of the delay is due to the need for all this processing. Hence the briefer forms of communication — cables, telexes — are preferable.

directory inquiries

Some people are put off by the absence of telephone directories in phone booths. There is no need to be. If you know the name and address of the person or organisation you want to contact, you can usually obtain the number by dialling 09. This service is heavily loaded in the daytime. Sometimes you get pips, which indicate you should hold the line till someone replies. Otherwise just keep dialling until you are lucky. And be ready with '*médlenno pozhálsta*' if the reply comes over too fast.

If you have the name and address in writing, you can hand it to the person in a street inquiry bureau (*správochnoye buró*) and for 2 kopecks obtain a written reply. But don't forget that a lot of people share a phone and your friend's may not be registered in his name.

The brevity and directness of Russian replies during business hours are often in marked contrast to their private manner. For instance, if you ask for Ivanov on his office line, you may hear just three syllables in reply — *on víshel*, which means not just 'he's gone out', as you might think, but 'he's gone out and will be back soon'. So there's no need to take offence, feel rebuffed, or ask when he will be back. Just try again in ten minutes or half an hour or whenever you feel 'soon' might be.

correspondence If you do have to write some letters, a few points are worth remembering. The letters you write to organisations such as the Ministry for Foreign Affairs or the Trade Ministry can be in English. But elsewhere delays at the other end can be avoided by getting letters translated and typed in Russian. There is a service for this at UPDK and the International Trade Centre. But if you have some Russian and know the form, you may prefer to rely on your own resources.

Here are a few standard letters that can be varied to meet your needs.

ПРОСЬБА ОСТАВИТЬ НОМЕР В ГОСТИНИЦЕ АНГЛИЙСКОМУ КОРРЕСПОНДЕНТУ 25-ГО ОКТЯБРЯ

(Telegram requesting reservation of a hotel room for a British correspondent.)

Директору государственного
Ордена Ленина Малого Театра

Уважансый господин директор!

Прошу Вас не отказать в любезности предоставить мне два билета на спектакль "Жизнь Клима Самгина". Я давно интересуюсь творчестаом Максима Горького и пишу диссертацию о нем.

С уважением

(Letter requesting two tickets for a Gorky play at the Maly Theatre on the grounds that the letter-writer is doing a thesis on Gorky.)

Директору издательства

Заявление

Прошу Вас предоставить мне справку о том, что я работал в издательстве штатным переводчиком с   по   1984 г.

(Letter requesting confirmation from director of a publishing house that you were employed as a staff translator for a specified period.)

У П Д К
Начальнику жилищного
отдела

Прошу Вас не отказать в любезности предоставить мне номер в гостинице в Завидово с   по
Номер моей машины

С уважением,

(Request for hotel accommodation at UPDK hunting lodge in Zavidovo. Note the polite opening, as in the letter to the director of the Maly Theatre.)

intercity phoning

Most cities in the Soviet Union are linked up by an STD system, but it would be rather a tall order for a beginner to obtain somebody's number in, say, Tashkent, and find out the code number of the city, how many digits have to be

filled in, and in what order to dial them all.
If you are living in a hotel, it's better to ask the
service bureau to obtain the number and get you
through. Russian speakers can go to an intercity
(*mezhdugoródny*) point, which is usually at or
next door to a post office, and ask to be put
through, but this may mean a long and uncomfortable wait.

Once you have the number and the code, you
can dial from the 15 kopeck *avtomát*, which is
also to be found in hotels and post offices. The
system for these is similar to the British. Your
15 kopecks gives you less time the further your
voice has to travel, and the phone warns you
that your time is running out with pips. On the
intercity, if you insert another 15 kopecks right
away, the connection will not be lost.

People who have their own phone can dial
from their flat on the same basis and the bill
arrives later. Dial 07 if you speak Russian. But
inquiries in English may be made on 8194, the
international telephone exchange.

Always pay any phone bills promptly, even
though they may be a long time coming. The
same applies to the monthly subscription.
You should pay several months in advance,
particularly if you go away for long periods.
The bills are usually quite small, but once your
phone is cut off it may take months to get it
restored.

international calls   If you are a private subscriber (i.e., have a home
telephone), it's quite easy to order a call to
Britain, the United States, or wherever, although
you should allow for a longish wait at times
when the lines are likely to be crowded, particularly Christmas.

In Moscow the number to dial is 8194. The
operator will answer in Russian and, if you want
to speak English, say *po-angléesky, pozhálsta,*

and wait till an English-speaking operator comes on the line. It's a good thing to know the code of the town you are calling. Even an experienced operator may be confused by such place-names as Loughborough, for instance. Pronounce any difficult name syllable by syllable and the operator will write down, in Russian, what it sounds like.

You can also call Britain or the United States from any other city on the Intourist routes by asking the service bureau in your hotel. For example, a call to Britain from Moscow or any other city in the Soviet Union costs 9 roubles for a minimum of three minutes and 3 roubles for each subsequent minute. The charge for a call from any Soviet city to anywhere in the United States is 6 roubles per minute with no obligatory minimum.

Business visitors can arrange for calls overseas to be charged to their company in Britain or the United States. Inquire of your local telephone manager before leaving. With a GPO card number, for example, you can also make credit card calls.

credit facilities

Telex is a good way of communicating with Britain, but not everybody has one. The Commercial Department of the British Embassy at Kutuzovsky Prospekt 7/4 makes its telex available to business visitors. Their telex number is 413341 and the answer back code is BEMOS SU. The current charge is £2 for the first three minutes and £1 per minute thereafter. Messages have to be collected or taken there for transmission by the person concerned. The US–USSR Trade and Economic Council will help American business people in the same way.

telex and telegrams

Not every little post office will take an international telegram, but most of the larger ones will. You ask for a *mezhdunaródny blank* (international message form) and print the name, address and message in block capitals in English. For some reason Soviet telegraphists like you to write Grande Bretagne, not Great Britain, in the space for country, but it doesn't really matter. At the bottom of the form there is a space for the sender's address. Have this written for you on a slip of paper, if you can't write in Russian, and the telegraphist will copy it in. From a hotel, of course, it's much simpler because the personnel are more experienced. The current rate to Britain is 30 kopecks a word (minimum 22 words). An urgent telegram costs twice as much, but an ordinary one gets there in a few hours anyway.

letters   Incoming letters may take anything from one to three weeks to arrive. Outgoing mail is rather quicker. One way of eliminating a little of the delay is to have your Russian address printed clearly in Russian in the right sequence, not forgetting the index number. The right sequence is: Country, city (plus district index number), street, house number, block (if any) and then the addressee's name. When someone sends you a letter with your address written in English and in the English manner, it has to be transcribed by post office workers into Russian on a label that is then stuck to the envelope, so that the postman can read it.

You can have mail sent to you *poste restante* at the Main Post Office, Kirov Street, or the Central Telegraph, Gorky Street (see the map on p. 179). Take your passport with you to collect.

When mailing letters to places within the USSR, the index number is also very important because sorting is done by an electronic scanner. For speed always use Soviet envelopes and follow the conventional number system indicated on the flap of the envelope. It is customary to write the sender's address in the space provided.

Parcels can be quite a problem. Parcels from abroad have to be collected from the International Post Office, which is quite a distance along the Varshavskoye Chaussée. They are examined for dutiable goods. Freight that has come in by road is collected at a depot along the same road, at the 26th kilometre, Butovo. All customs charges there have to be made in hard currency. Freight shipped in by rail is usually collected at the Central Customs in Komsomolskaya Square.

    If you want to post a parcel abroad, take whatever you are sending to the Main Post Office or the Central Telegraph, and show them what it is. If it can be sent, they will give you the forms to fill in, sell you a box or wrap the parcel as required, and ask you to write the address. All this takes time and you may need someone to help you. A preliminary visit to inquire about possible restrictions and collect the forms may be the best course.

parcels

Probably the only British newspaper you will be able to buy will be an occasional *Morning Star* at a hotel bookstall. Unless you want to forget it all for a while, take a short-wave transistor (19 m and 25 m) with you. BBC World Service and Voice of America reception is fairly good in Moscow. But you should also have with you a small aerial that you can dangle out of the window in case your hotel happens to have ferro-concrete walls, which block the signal.

    Some British newspapers and magazines can be read in the waiting room of the British embassy and the reading room of the embassy's cultural section. It should be possible to obtain copies of *The Times* in the Hotel Intourist in Gorki Street. Visiting Americans have access

**keeping in
touch**

to the US embassy club facilities. Back numbers of *The Times* and the *Times Literary Supplement* can be consulted with varying success in the files of the Lenin Library (Kalinina, 3) and the Foreign Languages Library (Ulyanovskaya, 1), if you have researcher status, i.e., hold a university degree. But this may have to be backed up by a letter from your organisation.

Soviet publishers put out quite a lot of informative material in English. The weekly *Moscow News*, and *MN Information* (twice weekly), are useful guides to what is going on locally. Apart from illustrated and political handouts, there is the more serious magazine *Soviet Literature*, which prints full-length novels, stories and plays by Soviet authors, and rather complex articles on literary subjects. Major works in hard cover are published in Moscow by Progress, Raduga and other Soviet publishers. The quality of the translation varies, but their lists include some important works of this and past centuries that are unobtainable in other editions. These are sold at various book shops in the big cities, the main ones in Moscow being at Zubovsky Bulevar 21, and Vesnina 8/10, which also carry a selection of Penguins, albeit at rather high prices. Russian–English and English–Russian dictionaries and other learning aids are published by Russian Language Publishers, sometimes jointly with Pergamon Press and Oxford University Press. But though printed in editions of as much as 100,000, they are quickly sold out on the home market. So it may be advisable to equip yourself before you start.

What's in a (Russian) Name?

forgetful
foreigners

Any Russian who has much to do with foreigners is used to them forgetting the second part of his or her name — the patronymic. For this reason they may soon suggest that you use only their first name. If you feel you can let them do the same to you, you may sail into a closer relationship with someone to whom you might have long remained a semi-stranger. But often the age or seniority gap is too wide for such informality and you will have to make an effort of memory. You will find it much easier to remember Russian names if you know how they are formed and what significance they have apart from just establishing a person's identity.

In any case, knowing the way Russians address each other tells you quite a lot about them and may help you to begin to unravel the mysteries of the national character.

Unlike us, Russians always have three, and only three, parts to their full name — the first or given name, the patronymic (derived from the father's name) and the family name (easy to remember the Russian for this because it sounds very much like 'family' — *fameeliya*).

use of
initials

Incidentally, Russians never use initials in speaking of a person, although it might appear from books and newspapers that they often do. A newsreader, for instance, will always find out, or be told, what the initials stand for and give the name in full. Initials are used in print as a sign of respect — and sometimes omitted to show disrespect. It is inconceivable that, for instance, any Russian writer could become widely known by his initials and surname, as

H. G. Wells or J. B. Priestley were in the West, although from scanning the Soviet press it might appear that all of them are.

first names and patronymics Popular first names for men are Iván, Vladéemir, Aleksándr, Yevgéni, Grigóri, Mikhaéel, Véektor, and a good many others. To make a male patronymic out of a male first name you simply add the ending 'ovich' or 'evich', depending on whether it ends in a consonant or a vowel. So the patronymic of Iván is Ivánovich, and when Iván is addressed formally he becomes 'Iván Ivánovich'. If his father's name had been Grigóri, he would be called Iván Grigórievich.

Similarly with women. Some of the well known names for women are Ánna, Alexsándra, Natálya, Antonína, Tatyána and Tamára. But instead of the masculine endings I have just mentioned, you add to a female first name the feminine 'ovna' or, if it ends in a vowel, 'evna'. So a Tamára whose father's name is Dmítri (pronounced 'Dmeetri') is formally addressed as Tamára Dmítrievna, meaning Tamára, daughter of Dmítri.

This patriarchal relic in a society where the family is by no means so large or cohesive a unit as it used to be is remarkable. It would even appear that the very forces of social change that shook the family have preserved its main symbol.

diplomatic form In diplomatic circles Russians speaking their own language to foreigners use the old Russian equivalent of Mr and Mrs — *gospodín* and *gospozhá* — and you can do the same to them. This is easy enough, but it's not quite so neutral as it sounds. Among ordinary Russians the title went out of use a long time ago and they would be very surprised, perhaps even offended, to hear themselves addressed by it. So what are you to call your next-door neighbour if he or she is about twenty years older than you? Again your

best course is to find out their name and
patronymic and try to remember them. This is
what Russians want to know, not your surname,
when they ask *Kak vas zuvoot?* — literally, 'How
are you called?' but meaning 'What shall I call
you?'

The most official form of address today is
'citizen' or 'citizenness' (*grazhdanéen* or *grazh-
dánka*). But this title with a name is reserved
almost exclusively for legal contexts. By itself
it is used mainly for calling someone to order,
reminding them that they have left something
behind, and so on. A rather more friendly form
is *továrishch* (comrade), and it is still widely
used. But *továrishch* along with somebody's
surname is rather formal. The official way of
addressing a superior in the army, for instance,
is *továrishch* plus his rank — *továrishch generál*,
továrishch serzhánt, and so on. You wouldn't
call your neighbour *továrishch Ivanóv*, for
instance. But by itself *továrishch* nowadays has
a nice friendly, slightly old-fashioned ring, not
half so political as 'comrade'.

továrishch

Of course, if you are in a situation in which
you can speak English all the time, you will
naturally use the English forms even to Russians,
and the Russians will gladly respond in kind.
They may make the mistake of calling you just
'mister' without your name or referring to 'Sir
so and so', using his surname instead of his first
name. But this should only alert you to how
funny your own mistakes in this sphere may
sound to them.

Let's assume, however, that you are working
on some project with Russians and picking up a
little of the language as you go along. If you are
too senior in rank or years to be addressed by
your first name, you may find someone calling
you *továrishch* Brown, Smith, or whatever.
But this would be thought of as taking rather a

liberty and anyone who tried would probably ask your permission first. A more natural alternative would be to ask what your father's name was and from this, without turning a hair, they would produce some extraordinary combination that would certainly ring strangely on your ears. If, for instance, you were named after your father 'John Brown', you might find yourself being called 'John Johnovich'. This may sound odd to you, but don't resist. It's a nice sign of respect and at the same time brings you closer to your colleagues. Incidentally, 'John' is the English equivalent of 'Ivan', but no one would ever russify you to the extent of calling you 'Iván Ivánovich'. One word of warning, however. Don't have your new-found patronymic entered on any forms (pay records, for instance), or one day an official may tell you they don't agree with what's written in your passport.

The longer you live in Russia the more you will appreciate the convenience of the halfway house between formality and informality that is provided by the use of the name and patronymic.

Another good reason for knowing about patronymics is that, though you may be on first-name terms with somebody fairly senior, there will be times when you have to ask for them on the telephone or refer to them in the presence of juniors. And for this the handiest form is 'Ánna Mikháilovna', 'Dmítri Ivánovich', and so on.

signing corres- pondence An interesting point is that the patronymic is never used in signing correspondence. Tamára Mikháilovna Pávlova, for instance, will sign herself 'Pávlova', even when writing to someone who always calls her Tamára Mikháilovna. So if you get a letter signed with just a surname, don't think you have suddenly fallen out of favour.

You may by now have the impression that Russians are very formal people and absolute sticklers for etiquette. But don't forget that not so long ago, within living memory, they swept away all the ranks and titles of the old empire and all the formalities connected with them. It would be nearer the truth to say that this clean sweep of formalities made people rather conscious of the value of those traditions that proved their worth and survived — and anxious to preserve them. There has even been talk of having some of the old ones back, such as *sóodar* (sir) and *soodárinya* (madam).

nicknames

The language Russians speak today is still enormously rich in nicknames, endearments, and endings that you can tack on to ordinary names to give them a special meaning — not all of them complimentary. While Johnny or Dicky is about as far as we can go from John and Richard, the Russians have three or four further gradations of affection that they can put into almost any first name. Aleksándra, a woman's name, or Aleksándr, a man's, for instance, can be Sásha, Shóora or Sánya for short, and any of these can apply to a woman or a man. They are all of equal value emotionally, and friends or relatives choose them as they will. But when Aleksándr was little, his mother probably called him *Sashóolya* or *Sáshenka* and, if he annoyed her, she would bark *Sáshka!* If she had chosen *Sánya*, he would at various times have been *Sanóolya*, *Sánenka* or *Sánka*. And Aleksandr's friends at school probably called him *Shura* or *Shóorik*, and in later years his wife may well have introduced further modifications.

Anyone who has ever tried to translate a Russian story or play knows what a problem the names are. Not only do the characters express their attitudes to each other through variations of name; the author himself at once shows a little of his attitude to any particular character and even tells you his or her approximate age and social status all in one or two words. It is an ingenious translator who can save the situation by tacking on 'love', 'dear', 'old', 'boy', and so on, in the right places.

name-days Some people still celebrate the 'name-day', which is not the same as a person's birthday, but the saint's day nearest to the day on which a person was born. Today it is seldom more than an occasion for a brief office party or a little family celebration. The days to remember are 30 September, when Vera, Nadezhda and Lyubov (Faith, Hope and Love) are the *imenéenniks*, heroines of the day, and 25 January, when Tatyána (Tánya, for short) gets a bit more attention than usual.

What all this adds up to is that in our computerised age the Russians are still exceptionally fond of names. With all those broad *o*s and *a*s, they roll off the tongue and Russians love to repeat a person's name in several of its different variants. So the least we can do is to remember who's who and what she or he likes to be called.

Suppose you have just taken over the bureau of a press agency. Before he retired, the previous head of the bureau, who spoke good Russian, called everybody by their first names, as he was perfectly entitled to do, having been on the job for such a long time. But you are twenty years younger. Perhaps there is someone who deserves a patronymic? Your driver, for instance, who is also near retiring age. But be careful with women's names. Even in Russia there are some who like to be known by their first names for ever and a day.

Shopping and Services

food

The Beryozka shops, which for hard currency offer most of the foods Westerners are used to, as well as Russian specialities such as caviare and sturgeon, have made shopping a lot easier for the foreign community in Moscow. But there are only two such shops that are open to all foreigners, one in the International Trade Centre on the Krasnopresnenskaya Embankment and the other in Dorogomilovskaya Street. A third, in Bolshaya Gruzinskaya, is reserved for people with D-series coupons, i.e., diplomats.

The hard-currency counters and department stores in the big hotels offer mainly drinks, sweets and other delicacies.

The Beryozka chain is even less noticeable in other cities. In the Ukraine it is known as Kashtan (chestnut-tree), presumably because there are so many chestnuts in Kiev. It may seem a bit of a mystery why these national symbols should be used to christen such exclusively foreign operations, until one considers the Union Jacks that blazon duty-free shops in the UK, for example.

'opportunity' shopping

Beryozka (or Kashtan) may be some distance from your home, so invest in a large fridge or a freezer to eliminate unnecessary travel. It will also come in useful when you find an ordinary shop round the corner where you can buy vegetables, eggs, milk, quick-frozen chickens, etc., without too much queuing. If you make friends with your neighbours or study the local *gastronóm* (grocery store) or *universám* (supermarket) yourself, you will gradually get to know when such items are most likely to appear. The times to avoid shopping are just before the lunch hour (which is between 1 and 2 p.m. for food shops and between 2 and 3 p.m. for others), and the rush hour from 5 to 7 p.m., when people are going home from work.

If you happen to be working for a Soviet organisation, you should inquire about the possibility of making a food order while you are at work. Many offices and factories have weekly deliveries of basic items with a few delicacies like salmon or caviare thrown in from time to time. These are made up into set orders. You choose which suits you best, pay for it, and collect it the following day before you go home.

Don't be misled into thinking that Moscow's sub-zero temperatures will keep everything frozen for you on the balcony, if you have one. Even in the coldest months there may be a thaw lasting several days that could leave you with a surplus of defrozen supplies.

at the market The markets you will find in most cities of any size are known as *kolkhózny* (collective farm) markets because this is where collective farmers and others sell any surplus they have grown or reared over and above what had to be delivered at state wholesale prices. Some experts call them 'free' markets, but the only free thing about them is the way prices go up with demand. There may be one or two state-run stalls selling meat or vegetables at controlled prices, but they don't have the supplies to compete with the individual producer, who puts his freshly killed veal or pork or out-of-season (from Central Asia) fruit on sale at four or five times the state price. The state intervenes in only one other area — all produce for sale at the market has to be passed by a state health inspector.

If you want the best cuts, you should go early, not later than ten. Weekends are the best times for shopping at market. The exception to this rule is Easter Sunday (Orthodox), which is still celebrated in the country. Russian Christmas Day (7 January equals 25 December by the old Calendar) is no time for marketing either. Markets are closed on public holidays, but just before them they are at their busiest.

Because of the high prices, people who shop at the market are rather choosy. They take any damaged fruit off the scales and expect to have it replaced. They eat the piece of apple offered as a sample, then pick out the best. The Antonovka, the autumn apple that keeps well through the winter, is usually selected in this way because people often buy in quantity, for storage.

You can follow their example but don't go to the length of passing from stall to stall sampling cherries and apricots, as some *nakhály* (impudents) do.

On the other hand, it's quite in order to walk away from a vendor who offers you salted cabbage that is too salty, or not crisp, or smells of fish (because the barrel wasn't scoured properly). As soon as the first frosts come, there is a big selection of salted cabbage at market and you choose what you like best by tasting the sample offered on a fork. People usually buy a kilo, which is forked out of a barrel into a plastic bag. If you buy that amount, you can ask for some additional *rassól* (fermented cabbage juice) and it will be poured into the bag along with the cabbage. When you get it home, pack the cabbage into a bowl, cover it and keep it in the fridge. Salted cucumbers, which come in earlier, are bought in the same way, and the brine is good for any member of the family who wakes up with a hangover.

There are all kinds of things on sale at the larger markets — from decorative plants to medicinal roots, and loofahs for scrubbing yourself in the bath. Except in winter, they are good places for flowers, especially when you are in urgent need and can't find anything at the florists'.

At some markets there is an overpowering smell of pickled garlic. On the whole the Russians don't use much garlic in their cooking, but they like to eat it raw or in their picklings. There is a belief that garlic is a good cure for colds, or at least a preventive. Probably the pickling does not enhance this effect, but the fashion seems to be gaining ground.

beating the queue

There are very few shops where you can pay directly at the counter. So you may have to queue at both the counter and the cash-desk. One way to get round this is to go with a friend and time things so that he or she brings you the *chek* (receipt) from the cash-desk before your turn comes up at the counter. When alone and in a hurry, get straight into whichever queue looks to be moving slower, wait for someone to join it behind you and ask him to keep your place. It's the accepted thing. Just point at your feet and say *pozhálsta*.

In shops that sell larger items, including shoes and clothes, you have to get a bill made out by the sales person. When you have paid it at the cash-desk, you go to a counter (*kontról*) near the exit, where your purchases are wrapped.

self-service

The introduction of self-service shops and the supermarket (*universám*) is making shopping a lot simpler.

Most hardware stores are partly self-service. For soap powders, saucepans, plastic buckets, etc., you can walk around with a basket choosing what you want, but for tools, screws, hinges and the like you have to be served. A point to remember is that most of these items are on show in display cases with the prices marked, so for something simple, like a screwdriver, don't join the crowd round the counter pestering the sales person with questions; find out the price and pay at the cash-desk first. In electrical shops, too, there is always a display board showing the power and price of the electric bulbs available.

Self-service is a boon for shoppers who don't know the language, and it's worth finding out where the best self-service shops are. Remember always to take one of the shop's baskets (some shops insist on your surrendering your own at a special counter) and don't be surprised if your purchases are checked against your receipt before you leave. When you are at the cash-desk, watch the cash register to find out how much you have to pay rather than rely on what the cashier says, which you may not be able to catch.

Most department stores (*univermåg*) have now been reorganised on a help-yourself basis. You pick out the jacket or hat you want and take it to the girl on duty in your section, who makes out a bill and has your purchase wrapped while you pay for it at the cash-desk. **department stores**

Raincoats, jackets, suits and so on are usually arranged so that you can pick them out and try them on yourself. If you don't feel equal to asking the price (*tsená*), try studying the label inside, where it is printed, sometimes rather illegibly, along with the name of the maker, country or origin, quality grade, and size.

It's not really worth going into the question of sizes, except to say that they differ from English and are not quite the same as 'continental' either. For intance, a Soviet size 42 shoe (English size 9, US size 10½) equals a 43 continental. At present Soviet suits and jackets are graded in five lengths, no. 5 being the longest. But the whole system is being revised and, in any case, you can usually try on coats and shoes without having to state what size you need. **sizes**

Compared with other things in the Soviet Union, clothes and footwear are expensive. There used to be a huge gap between the prices of shoes in Britain and the USSR. As Western prices have risen, the gap has narrowed, but it's still too wide to make regular buying practical, unless you have a large supply of roubles and very little currency. But the variety of clothes and shoes is much larger than it used to be. Most of the Comecon (Russians call it SEV) countries have opened shops in Moscow, and so has India. Clothes are also being imported from Finland, France and West Germany. So you may well be able to meet an immediate need in a Moscow shop.

international trade centre The big complex on the Krasnopresnenskaya Embankment offers for any hard currency (*valyúta*) food, clothing, footwear, jewellery, airline tickets, radios, Soviet books, china, and banking facilities. There are also bars, restaurants, and a heated swimming pool. At present the range of goods is not very large and they don't stock everyday things, but it's all under one roof and very pleasant.

commission shops In most cities there are *komíssiónny* shops, selling all kinds of things, from works of art to collapsible boats. They are rather like our second-hand shops, though some of the goods sold there are brand new. Russians frequent them for the same reasons as we go to ours — for something out of the ordinary, for bargains, and just for curiosity's sake. Their addresses and phone numbers are all listed in the useful 1983 Moscow telephone directory (*správochnik*). Only Soviet people may sell things through them.

art and antiques In Moscow and other cities there are art galleries and shops that sell contemporary works of art, antiques, old paintings and furniture, crystal, china, ceramics, bronze ornaments, and so on. Some of them are also run on a commission basis. The gallery or shop undertakes to sell the owner's property for a commission. If it is not sold, the gallery may, with the owner's consent, reduce the price. Nothing is kept in the shop for more than a few months. The display constantly changes and such shops are worth visiting. But the recent introduction of severe restrictions on the export of all objects made before 1945 has made the purchase of antiques or even semi-antiques pointless for visitors, although it has brought the prices down for Russians.

Most contemporary work can be exported duty-free if you keep the receipt from the gallery, but on some items you may need an export licence and have to pay export duty. Even paintings that are given to you have to be valued and duty may be charged. The object itself and two photographs of it have to be submitted when you apply.

In all cases make a serious inquiry before buying. The address of the Export Commission is Chekhova 29 (tel. 221 32 58) and they are open only from 10.30 to 2 p.m. on Tuesdays.

books, souvenirs, records, music

The regulations concerning the export of literature are as strict as for art. Nothing published before 1966 can be taken out without permission. The current regulation concerning literature published after that date declares that one-volume dictionaries, books in foreign languages, children's literature, textbooks, Braille books, Marxist political literature, and some works of the natural and social sciences do not require an export permit. This all applies to anything mailed abroad as well.

The procedure for obtaining permission to export outside these categories (e.g., old or limited editions) is tedious. It involves making up a list of the books with all their particulars and visiting a department of the Lenin Library (tel. 203 14 19) on the right day (Monday or Friday, from 1 to 4 p.m.).

Books and other items purchased at the Beryozka shops (International Trade Centre, and Kropotkinskaya 31) may be exported without permission but you must remember to retain the shop's receipt, any markings on the book, and its label.

At present there are no restrictions on the export of records and music.

GUM   In Moscow the main department store is GUM (pronounced *'goom'*), which is really three huge shopping arcades on two levels. It is located just off Red Square. For an overall view of the shopping situation other than food you can't do better than pay it a visit. The best time to go shopping at GUM is late Saturday afternoon when less people are about.

If you have some knowledge of Russian (and a quick ear), you can even try making use of the phones at the corners of connecting passages for inquiring what is where. Don't waste words. Just say what you want — gloves, swimming trunks, headscarf or whatever — and listen carefully for the reply, which will be equally short and sharp, directing you to the right row (*léeniya*) and floor (*etage*). An important landmark in this shopping maze is the central fountain (French again, *fontán*).

After an hour or two you may decide that there were some things, such as tampons, toilet paper, rufflette tape, buttons, cottons and nail scissors, that you should have brought with you. But the shopping situation changes so unpredictably that advice is difficult to give. A few years ago there wasn't a teapot or a brief-case to be had in Moscow. Now the place is full of them. Pillows have lately become more plentiful, but most of them are much bigger than ours.

If you badly needed a cushion you could buy some material and go to an upholsterer's (*remónt mébeli*) and ask them to make it up for you. They would probably oblige or tell you of some other workshop (*masterskáya*) that would do it.

On the whole, it is better to adapt yourself to Russian things than to import as soon as the need arises. For instance, a fast-boiling British electric kettle may blow all the fuses on your staircase. English lampshades, though very pretty, have rings that are too small. Some American dictation machines have opposite wiring from that of Soviet (and British) systems. VHF bands differ from the Soviet, which range from 65 to 73 MHz. But if you do get stuck with a problem of this kind it's worth trying one of the local workshops.

Some of their usual functions are to duplicate your keys, fit bindings to skis, bind books, make your vacuum cleaner work, mend your jacket, and so on. Some districts have places where all these services are brought together under one roof (*kombinát*). There are also people who do repairs privately.

Russian friends will often give you invaluable advice on this score. But beware of the eager genius. All over the world there are people who long to get their screwdrivers into any piece of equipment they have never seen before, and yours may never be quite the same again. Make sure you have a reliable recommendation for the repair man (*máster*) who services your typewriter or tape-recorder.

If you are a diplomat, in business or a newspaper correspondent permanently based in Moscow,

máster and masterskáya

UPDK

the place you go to for all your basic needs is UPDK, which stands for Diplomatic Corps Service Bureau (or Board). It's an important organisation and its director has the diplomatic status of an ambassador. It caters for two or three thousand diplomats and anyone else accredited with the Ministry for Foreign Affairs, providing flats, domestics, interpreters, and so on.

letters to UPDK

Letters to UPDK if in Russian, should be couched in formal diplomatic language (see page 45). It's better to write in Russian. Letters in other languages are sent to a translation department and this will delay the response.

booking through UPDK

As I have already suggested, a preliminary phone call may save you trouble. For instance, the procedure for booking accommodation at the Zavidovo Hunting Lodge is as follows. You phone the appropriate department of UPDK (201 27 17) and ask if a room or a chalet is available on such and such a date. If it is, you will be asked to bring them a letter of request at a time of your own choosing. Ask for the department's internal phone number and call them from the lobby of the main building (Kropotkinskaya 21) when you get there. A person will then come down to the waiting room, read your letter and write an instruction on it. You then take the letter to another building, about half a mile away (Kursovoy 1), pay the bill and receive your *putyóvka* (travel voucher). Once the letter is written, the rest can, of course, be done by your driver, if you have one.

For more important negotiations, definite appointments have to be made at the appropriate level. But for small requests, such as stationery orders, repairs to your fridge, etc., a letter taken to Kursovóy Street should be sufficient. Bills charged in hard currency are usually paid through one's account at the Foreign Trade Bank.

UPDK has a small but rather efficient repair garage for its clients near the Kiev Station (Kievskaya 8, tel. 240 20 92). They handle foreign makes but any parts required have to be imported by the owner. The same can be said for No. 7 station, near the National Achievements Exhibition (Selkhokhozyáistvenny Proyezd 6, tel. 181 06 31), which specialises in German makes. The Volvo car company recently opened a large and fully equipped service station for its cars. Manned by Soviet mechanics, it is fairly well supplied with spares and can also have parts sent in direct from Sweden, which is cheaper and more convenient than ordering them oneself. This service is located near the intersection of the Minsk and circular roads (Gorbunovskaya 14, Entrance 5, tel. 448 80 35).

car repairs

The car breakdown service can be called during the day on 119 80 00 and 119 81 08.

emergencies

These may vary with the climate — shops open earlier in the south. In Moscow, food shops (dairies, bakers, grocers, greengrocers, etc.) open at 8 a.m. Most of them close from 1 to 2 p.m. for lunch, but in a few cases the lunch break is from 2 to 3 p.m. Food shops usually stay open till 8, and some keep going till 9 p.m. Prepared food shops (*koolinaríya*) are open from 8 a.m. till 9 p.m. with a lunch break from 2 to 3 p.m.

Hardware shops open at 10 a.m., but some stationery and haberdashery shops do not begin until 11 a.m. Their lunch break is from 2 to 3 p.m., and they close at 7 or 8 p.m.

The big department stores, GUM, Moskva and

opening and closing times

Children's World (*Détsky Mír*), are open all day from 8 a.m. to 9 p.m. without a break.

The diplomats' *gastronóm* (B. Gruzinskaya) is open from 10 a.m. to 1 p.m. and from 2 to 7 p.m., whereas the Dorogomilovskaya hard-currency *gastronóm* trades from 9 a.m. to 7 p.m. with a break from 2 to 3 p.m.

All hardware and department stores are closed on Sundays, but quite a number of food shops open as usual but close two hours earlier than on weekdays. Hairdressers usually work all day in two shifts, from 8 a.m. to 9 p.m.

Garages and repair shops work from 8 a.m. to 8 p.m. with a break from 1 to 2 p.m. (UPDK garage, 2 to 3 p.m.). But to get a garage to do something for you on the same day you should go early.

Markets trade without a break from 7 a.m. to 6 p.m.

Small repair shops (*masterskáya*) may be closed on certain weekdays as well as Sundays. Small post offices often work mornings or afternoons only on alternate days.

Shops and many other establishments close for a 'cleaning day' (*sanitárny den*) about once a month, and shops may turn out to be closed for stock-taking (*na oochót*) at unpredictable times.

Getting About

If you are staying in the USSR for any length of time, you should try to get about as much as possible. With so many people saying Russia's a terrible place and so many others saying the opposite, your perceptions will certainly be heightened and the merest hint — an expression on a face, a friendly gesture — may mean a lot to you.

restrictions

There are restrictions, but don't let them reduce you to a state of apathy. For instance, unless you are an ambassador, you can't go more than 40 kilometres from the centre of Moscow without permission (see the next section on permissions). But permission is readily granted to visit places of interest well beyond this limit, such as the monastery town of Zagorsk, Tchaikovsky's home at Klin, and Borodino, the famous battlefield. Similar rules, and exceptions, apply in other cities.

Official instructions state that your arrival in any new place has to be reported to the local authorities within 48 hours. Usually this involves nothing more than handing in your passport at the hotel where you are staying. But if you are staying with friends, don't neglect the formalities.

permissions

At present there are over 140 Soviet cities on Intourist itineraries, which extend to all of the fifteen republics. A glance at an Intourist brochure will give you an idea of what places it would be easy to obtain permission to visit, but other requests are considered and sometimes granted. Diplomats and correspondents and accredited business representatives apply to the Ministry for Foreign Affairs; others to the foreign relations department (*otděl vněshnikh snoshěniyiy*) at their place of study or work. Always leave time for the official wheels to start turning, and keep your travel plans flexible.

student travel At present, individual travel for Western students is rather limited, except for any trips envisaged as part of the course. The Soviet university authorities have a strong belief in the value of attending lectures and making full use of their study facilities. They will certainly find it hard to understand someone who comes 2,000 miles to attend a course and then wants to miss most of the lectures. It's important to understand this insistence on taking what's on offer, though it may go against the grain for someone used to, say, the free-and-easy ways of British university life.

British students studying in cities other than Moscow can make occasional visits to the capital on the invitation of the consul or the cultural attaché at the embassy, and the university authorities will sometimes allow individual trips or arrange an excursion if a group can be got together. But as a rule students are expected to stay within university bounds while the course lasts.

What about booking a trip through Intourist to somewhere in the Soviet Union for when the course is over? The snag here is that it will probably mean forfeiting your share of the British Council's group ticket that takes you back to England as soon as the course ends. In summer one fairly cheap and enjoyable alternative might be to book a passage on a Soviet boat from Leningrad, if you can coordinate sailing times and visa expiry dates.

Intourist, Aeroflot and Morflot usually want to be paid in hard currency, but a student who has saved, or perhaps earned, roubles during his stay has a good case for using them to pay his fare home. Apply to Intourist with a letter from whatever organisation paid you.

Booking accommodation in advance is important. A booking is usually made by sending a reply-paid telegram to the hotel in question. Make sure you have a confirmation because there may be no alternative but to come back the same day if no accommodation is available. UPDK, the Diplomatic Corps Service Bureau (202 28 65), or your foreign relations department can do this for you.

accommodation

Hotel accommodation is cheap, but only for people living on a Soviet salary, i.e., Soviet citizens or foreigners working for Soviet organisations. Diplomats, correspondents and business people travelling individually pay a rate that has been brought into line with hotels in the more expensive Western countries. If you are working for a Soviet company, you should ask them to supply you with a letter confirming this fact and requesting that you be charged the ordinary Soviet rates. It will save you a lot of money. If, as a student, you have managed to earn some roubles by, say, making translations for a Soviet publisher or magazine, you should also explore this possibility.

Unless you own or hire a car (see pp. 79ff.), you will be using buses, trolleybuses, trams and the Metro (Underground, Subway) to get about town. The quickest and most convenient, particularly in winter, is, of course, the Metro (indicated by a large letter M on the ground-level entrance or entrances). Moscow, Leningrad, Kiev, Tashkent and Minsk have Metro systems and a start has been made on one for Tbilisi, capital of Georgia.

using public transport

paying the fare   On buses, trolleybuses, and trams there are no conductors to collect fares and you are expected to serve yourself with a ticket. There is a box at either end of the vehicle. You drop your money in and tear off a ticket from the attached roll. If you don't have the right value of coin, put in more and claim the difference off the next person to come aboard before he puts his in. When the bus or tram is crowded, you have to somehow raise your arm and ask the person next to you to pass on your money to the box, tear off a ticket and pass it back to you. If you are standing near the box yourself, you will find quite a lot of coins coming your way and will have to drop them in and tear off the requisite number of tickets to pass back. This is rather an amusing experience for the newcomer, but mind you don't miss your stop, particularly in winter, when bus and tram windows are all frosted up. Try to remember the number of stops on your route, so that you don't have to make out what the driver is calling out over the intercom.

lucky number   When there's nothing to do on a long bus ride, add up the first three figures on your ticket, then the last three. If the sums are equal, keep the ticket. Russians say it will bring you luck. But don't start whistling a tune. Russians of the older generation don't like whistling — they think it's a sound that makes money disappear.

Urban transport in Moscow is charged at a flat rate — 5 kopecks take you all the way by tram, trolleybus, bus or Metro. If you have run out of change or just want to have tickets in reserve, you can buy a little book of ten from the driver while at a stop. What you do then is take one out of the book and drop it into the box instead of a coin, then tear off a different ticket from the roll attached to the box. Some buses have little clipping machines as well as boxes. In this case you take a ticket out of your book and clip it in the machine, then keep it to show any inspector who comes aboard; he's entitled to fine you if you haven't got a properly clipped ticket, but probably won't.

Peak travel times are between 7 and 9 a.m., and 5 and 7 p.m., so it's obviously better to avoid them if you can.

Metro

The Metro also gets crowded at rush hours. But trains are so frequent that even the most formidable platform jam is quickly sucked away. Besides being warm and well ventilated, the Metro has the advantage that you don't have the same trouble with fares. You simply press a 5 kopeck piece into a slot at the top of the escalator, a gate opens and you can travel without further payment until you come up to the surface. There is a diagram of the system in the hall of every station and in each coach, and of the particular line you are on along the walls facing the platforms. With a few 5 kopeck pieces in your pocket you can make quite extensive tours of five major Soviet cities and see some interesting architectural interiors as well.

suburban trains

The Metro will take you out to several places in the suburbs with less chance of confusion than if you travel from a large railway terminal. But if you have enough command of the language to read signboards and timetables, you can try a suburban train journey.

The first thing is to get a ticket. Again you serve yourself, usually from a slot machine. There will be a board in the booking office, listing the stations and which fare zones they are in. Look up the station you want, insert the right number of coins in the machine and you get your ticket.

Make sure you know which line your station is on, and that the train stops at that station (fast trains often miss several). The platform gate will have a sign over it showing the departure time and the train's final destination. You don't have to show your ticket. Just get aboard and have it ready in case a collector comes round. The coaches in suburban trains are not compartmented. The corridor runs down the centre with seats on either side. You can smoke only at the end of the corridor, beyond the sliding doors.

Soviet surburbs are far more countrified than we are used to. At a station only ten miles from the centre of Moscow you might have to choose one of several paths through a sizeable wood to reach the house you are looking for. So arrange to be met at the station.

finding an address   Even if you have some knowledge of the language, it is best to get any address you need to find clearly printed in Russian on a slip of paper that you can show to a taxi driver, fellow passenger or passer-by. It's also a good idea to have the friend you are visiting meet you at his bus-stop or the nearest Metro station, especially if he lives in one of the new housing developments, where large apartment blocks are clustered at various angles to the street to avoid traffic noise and other disturbances. Metro stations often have two exits on different sides of a wide street or square, so make sure you know which one is meant.

Russian addresses are written in the reverse order to ours. First comes the town and postal code, followed by the district, the street (улица or ул.), the house number (дом or д.), the block (кориус or К.), if it is one of a cluster, the apartment number (кь.), and finally the name of the addressee. Two large tower blocks may come under one house number and be distinguishable only by a large letter A or B etc., painted on one wall. This is indicated in the address as кориус A, Б, and so on. If you are visiting, you

will also need to know the number of the
entrance (some blocks have as many as fourteen)
and the floor (*étage*). What English people call
the ground floor is the first floor to the Russians
as it is to Americans, and so on upwards.

Sometimes it is important to know the
different kinds of streets, lanes, etc. There is,
for instance, in Moscow a Kropótkinskaya
úlitsa (street) and a Kropótkinsky *pereúlok*
(lane). There is a Bolsháya (big) Gruzinskaya
and a Málaya Gruzínskaya *úlitsa* (Little Gruzin-
sky Street). And these variants may not necessarily be very close to each other. Some streets
with the same name are numbered 'first'
(*pérvaya*), 'second' (*vtoráya*), and so on. If a
name ends in 'aya', it is probably a street, but
it may also be an embankment (*náberezhnaya*).
The following list with standard abbreviations
may help:

Russian	*Pronounced*	*English*
шоссе́, ш.,	chaussée	highway, main road
проспе́кт, просп.	prospékt, prusp.	avenue
бульва́р, бульв.	bulvár, bulv.	boulevard
на́бережная, наб.	náberezhnaya, nab.	embankment
вал	val	wall
у́лица, ул.	óolitsa, ul.	street
переу́лок, пер.	pereóolok, per.	lane, side-street
прое́зд, пр.	proyézd, pr.	drive
тупи́к	toopéek	cul de sac
пло́щадь, пл.	plóshchad, pl.	square
больша́я, Б.	bulsháya, B.	big, great
ма́лая, М.	málaya, M.	little

Your friend's house may have a front door that
is kept locked and can only be opened by
pressing a series of buttons. The door is often
left open, but ask him what his code (*kawd*) is,
just in case.

photography   Whether travelling about or staying put, you will probably want to use your camera. Some of the regulations on this score seem to date back to well before the age of electronics and earth satellites, but the fact remains that you are not allowed to take photographs from the air, or of anything, such as bridges, that might be of military importance. One has also to remember that people don't always like being photographed, particularly when they are not ready for it. So when in doubt, ask permission (*fotografĕerovat mózhno?*). And take plenty of film — you may not be able to find the kind you need on the spot.

taxis   The answer to some of your transport problems if you are not feeling active or are in a hurry may be a taxi. They are not widly expensive and can be ordered by phone. (In Moscow the best numbers are 225 00 00 and 227 00 40). But the lines are often engaged, English is not spoken, and you need to explain where you are to be picked up. The current change for taxis is 20 kopecks a kilometre added to the initial 20 kopeck charge. Most taxi drivers expect a tip nowadays, especially if they have had to ask around to find your address for you or help with luggage, which is not charged extra. A cargo-carrying (*groozovóy*) taxi can be ordered on 256 90 03.

Taxis have a chequered band round the body and a chequered orange sign on the roof. Taxi ranks are marked with a capital T and you can also sometimes stop taxis in the street if the green light on the windscreen is showing. Drivers may stop but refuse to take you, pointing to the time printed on a notice above the dashboard. They mean that their shift is over and their garage is not in your direction. This often happens around midnight. So, if you intend to burn the midnight oil with friends, ask them to phone for a taxi while you still have an hour or two to spare. This could save you some discomfort on a winter's night.

In some spots, at airports, for instance, or outside some of the big hotels, freelance drivers will offer you their services. They are best avoided because they nearly always try to overcharge you. But if you do have to take one, make sure how much he wants before you start.

Transport in the USSR is so cheap that even on a modest salary you can think of journeys of thousands of miles when planning a tour. Moscow—Samarkand, for instance, costs 56 roubles and you can fly from Moscow to Khabarovsk (6,000 miles) for 130. The same journey by rail on the Trans-Siberian, which offers a good way of seeing the country and people, takes six and a half days and costs about the same, not counting the price of your meals. So if you are short of time, you can do part of the journey by air.

longer journeys

A train journey across Russia can be a fascinating experience. The distances are great, the speeds, except on a few routes, not very high, and the whole atmosphere is rather relaxing, if you like that kind of thing. Most compartments are four-berthed and you will probably have companions, some of whom you may get to know quite well by the time the journey is over. There is no segregation of sexes, but sometimes men and women sort themselves out into separate compartments. If not, the usual thing is for the men to step into the corridor while the women are going to bed or getting up.

Glasses of tea and other refreshments come round at rather irregular intervals and there is usually a restaurant car. During stops you may have time to get out and buy local produce, but wise travellers take a good supply of food and drink with them. Something exotically British,

American, etc. from a flask or a bottle is sure to be appreciated by others in the compartment.

The grading of Soviet rail tickets can be slightly confusing. The old distinction between 'myagkhy' (soft) and 'zhostky' (hard) has disappeared with the passing of wooden seats. For long rail journeys nowadays you will be offered a choice between a berth in a two-berth sleeper and one in a four-berth. The two-berth compartment is more roomy, better upholstered and costs more. A berth in a two-berth or four-berth compartment is called 'kupeiny' (compartmented) to distinguish it from the next grade down, which is 'obshchiy' (general). In both cases you are provided with a mattress, bed linen, pillow and blankets. If there is nothing going in the two top grades you may be offered a 'platskartny', which means a reserved berth in a general coach. This is very cheap but lacking in conveniences, although the reservation includes bedding as in the others.

Some fast trains have lounge-type coaches. Sitting in one of these, you can do the 500 miles from Moscow to Leningrad in six hours. But you can also make an overnight journey of it, in a comfortable sleeper, in which case you pay 24 roubles instead of 19.

Don't forget that journeys often have to be booked well ahead. At least nine days should be allowed for the Trans-Siberian route.

time factor On some routes it is hard to decide whether air will be more convenient than rail, or even quicker. In winter, apart from the time wasted getting to and from airports, planes are sometimes grounded for a day or more by fog or snowstorms, which seldom affect rail traffic.

If stuck at a crowded airport, always go to the Intourist section, whether or not you are travelling with them, and they will do what they can to get you accommodation.

Driving, Owning and Hiring a Car

Driving in the Soviet Union may sometimes remind you of the halcyon early days of motoring. There are few parking problems and most roads are relatively uncrowded. But the situation is rapidly changing. More and more private cars are coming on the road, and to the fairly heavy weekday flow of truck traffic round the big cities has been added the continental container lorry and the fast intercity bus. Motorways are being developed but at present do not extend more than twenty miles from the larger cities. Most main roads are dual- or treble-laned without a dividing mid-road barrier.

When touring therefore you can expect long stretches of easy driving with glorious views of forested or steppeland country, interrupted by sudden patches of bad road or the equally sudden honk of an intercity bus that has crept up behind you and wants to get past. Since the bus-driver will be going as fast as it is safe to go on that road, it is better to reduce speed and let him get well ahead rather than try to leave him behind, even though your car may have far greater power of acceleration.

Some of the brochures for foreign motor tourists are not very clear and a bit off-putting. They really ought to be presented in a simpler form. I quote: 'Travel through towns without a stop-over is not allowed.' What this means is that you are not allowed to skip the overnight stop that will have been booked for you at the hotel or camping site on your itinerary.

touring

Nowadays you can't just drive on through the night and sleep in the car when you get tired.

The most important rule is that you have to stick closely to the itinerary you have chosen out of those offered by Intourist — the present selection covers just over 10,000 km. If you decide to change your itinerary en route, you can do this by agreement with the nearest Intourist office. It will entail paying ten per cent of the cost of the unused part of your first itinerary over and above the cost of the new one.

formalities On entering the country with a car there are several formalities to go through. You will be given a sketch map of your route and a form to fill in known as the Motor Tourists' Memo, stating your name, vehicle licence number, itinerary, and so on. At the customs you will have to sign a declaration undertaking to take the car out of the country. Keep all these in a handy place along with your international driving licence, certificate of vehicle registration, passport and exit visa, so that you can show them when required.

During these procedures you can avoid delay by knowing where all the various numbers on your car actually are. For instance, the customs man may want to check the engine number and perhaps the chassis number, too, but he may not know where to find them on your particular make of vehicle.

If you have only a national driving licence, you can get it validated for the Soviet Union at the Intourist border crossing point.

insurance Insurance is not compulsory for Soviet private motorists. For this reason alone (you or your car might be damaged by someone without insurance) it is vital to take out full coverage, including third party. If you have not done this before leaving home, it can be arranged at the border, where there will be agents of the state insurance company known as Ingostrakh. Ingostrakh works on the principle that compensation is paid in the same currency as the premium.

Don't forget that border point officials have ordinary working hours like everybody else. Plan your journey so that you arrive at the border at a reasonable time of day.

fuel

If your car runs on very high octane fuel, you may need to have your ignition slightly advanced to cope with a lower grade. Vouchers marked 98 octane are sold, but nearly everywhere the highest grade available is 95 or 96. All petrol with an octane number of 93 and over currently costs 40 kopecks a litre. Tourists are expected to buy vouchers for their whole trip at the border. If for some reason you fail to complete the itinerary, you can claim your money back from the travel agent who arranged your trip.

Vouchers for the grade of petrol known as Extra (95 octane) can be purchased from UPDK (Kursovoy 1, except on Fridays) and the Ukraine Hotel. Soviet cars run on 93 and 76 octane fuels, which are available at most fuel stations. The number of stations selling petrol for cash is increasing over those that will accept only vouchers. The ratio in Moscow at present is about 4 to 1 in favour of cash. But it's wise to have vouchers with you, in case you hit a bad patch. They are on sale at tobacconists' kiosks and hardware stores and some cash-accepting fuel stations will also sell you vouchers. For the Extra grade you need vouchers and they must have the stamp of your embassy, newspaper or company on the back.

At fuelling stations you serve yourself after paying or handing in your vouchers at a box-office, from which the flow of fuel is controlled.

taking care   The rest can be summed up in a few words —
drive carefully, especially if you are not used to
driving on the right-hand side of the road. When
you are in traffic, you are not likely to forget
which side you should be on. It's after a party,
or a picnic lunch by a deserted road, that you
are liable to drive out on to the wrong side.

The shoulders of even main roads are often
rather soft. So be cautious about pulling off,
especially after rain.

Long distances may make you impatient,
but even on deserted roads don't do more than
90 kmph (55 mph). An apparently good surface
can give you a sudden, hair-raising bump where
it has either bulged or subsided owing to
extremes of temperature.

In villages and small towns the 60 kmph
(37 mph) speed limit is quite justified because
cats, chickens and cyclists can appear quite
unexpectedly in front of your wheels. After
a long spell at ninety, sixty will seem like
crawling. But be prepared to go slowly if the
road signs tell you to.

Intourist has a good point about not trying
to drive more than 500 km in a day, and
avoiding night driving. But the days shorten
rapidly in September and you may find yourself still on the road after nightfall.

night driving   Despite traffic regulations, some Soviet drivers
still prefer to use their sidelights instead of
dipped headlights — and expect you to do the
same. Don't follow their example. You need
dipped headlights to show up pedestrians,
cyclists and farm wagons on the right-hand
verge. Cyclists rarely have a rear light and
sometimes not even a reflector.

British and American drivers should ensure
that their headlights have been adjusted for
driving in continental Europe. Otherwise they
may be angled at the middle of the road.

Long straight roads make you sleepy, even during the day, so stop frequently and take a little walk, but not where there's a no-stopping sign.

The Russians use accepted international road **road signs** signs and there are few directions or warnings written out in words. This is convenient for the foreigner with no Russian. But the traffic people are not particularly lavish with their

cautionary signs either. A single exclamation mark may be the only warning you will get of a dual carriageway ahead.

They also use pictographs, not words, for advising you of available services. Very easy when you get used to them and saves you a language problem. But there doesn't seem to be a road sign for toilets. Perhaps no one has been able to decide what picture would be applicable to the local loos. Once you have stopped, you may notice two doors with the Russian letters M and Ж or pictograms distinguishing the gents' and the ladies'. Both interiors, however, are likely to be devoid of toilet paper.

When you are in contact with Intourist, always ask them how to find the hotel or camping site at your next stopover. The camping site sign is just an iconic tent, and it's easy to miss it in failing light.

driving points

In the cities, circular and arterial roads are usually wide — the main circular in Moscow, for instance, averages five lanes each way. This prevents congestion, but it presents one or two problems for drivers who are used to a smaller scale.

You may have difficulty in spotting the traffic lights, which are often way off to the side of you or strung up very high in the middle of the road.

lane driving

Traffic lanes are not always clearly marked, so you have to be especially wary of the driver who likes to zigzag through traffic. Where they are marked, a broken line can be crossed and a solid line should not be crossed except in an emergency. Double lines or 'reserve areas' down the centres of roads are even more prohibitive.

You are not supposed to stay in the outside, left-hand lane when other lanes to your right are vacant. But in town keep clear of the kerbside lane until you are actually going to stop or turn right, or you will have to steer round stopping trolleybuses and parked vehicles — a point to remember in winter, when it's slippery.

A traffic policeman stationed in the middle of the road may wave urgently at you if you stay in the left-hand lane. This usually means that he wants you to make way for a VIP car coming up fast behind you. Comply promptly but not so promptly that you bump into someone on your right. The latest generation of Russian drivers seems to cling rather stubbornly to what they consider their rightful place on the road, even if you are signalling to move across.

A British driver may resent what he thinks of as 'passing on the inside' or the 'blind side'. Actually this is only illegal if the overtaker changes lanes to do so. But drivers often do just this with impunity and you have to be on the look-out for it. If the traffic in your lane suddenly slows down or stops, never change lanes until you are sure there is no one coming up behind.

The official speed limit in town is 60 kmph (37 mph). When the lanes are crowded, cars in the left-hand lane often go much faster than this and you can do the same. But on a clear road, you may be stopped and cautioned if you are exceeding the speed limit. **speed limit**

You may have to go some distance before finding a place where you can turn left or turn round. Quite a lot of streets in Soviet cities are laid out like boulevards, with tree-lined walks down the middle. If friends are explaining how to reach their place, check with them on where you can make the necessary U-turns. **U-turns**

A tricky turning situation arises in the centre of Moscow, opposite the Bolshoi theatre. When approaching from the Kremlin side, you are confronted with a signpost sending you to the right for Gorky Street, and left for Dzerzhinsky Square. Actually the street lies to the left and the square to the right, but you are diverted to enable you to get into the right lane for the subsequent turn into Gorky Street without cutting across the stream. Incidentally, the best way to reach the car park at the Bolshoi Theatre is to take the Gorky Street direction but turn right before you get there, at Pushkin Street, then right again.

Trams sometimes have special side-lanes reserved for them. You may not drive in these **trams** and can only cross them at certain points. But you can cross tramlines down the middle of the road anywhere that is a safe distance from crossroads, unless there is a straight-on sign (white arrow on blue). Such signs operate as far as the next turning or intersection.

Keep your eyes open for trams, especially in Leningrad. On those magnificent squares a tram may suddenly appear, apparently out of nowhere, just when you are looking for some historic building. In wider streets you are permitted to pass a stationary tram at slow speed, but if there is no mid-road waiting area for passengers, you must stop to allow them to get on and off.

intersections You can turn right when the traffic lights show green, if there is no side arrow. If there is one, wait for it to light up before turning.

At equal intersections the driver with no vehicle on his right has the right of way — in other words, give way to traffic on your right.

crossings Nothing more than the behaviour of pedestrians crossing a street will convince you that the Russians are not the regimented people they are sometimes made out to be. When the green arrow gives you the right of way and your progress is barred by a stream of pedestrians pouring across the street against the red light, just edge forward politely into the thick of it. The chances are that you and your car will come out unscathed.

There are no zebra crossings of the UK kind where a pedestrian's foot on the road can bring the traffic to a screeching halt. You are expected to reduce speed at pedestrian crossings sufficiently to allow you to stop at once in an emergency. Few drivers do this, but some pedestrians behave as if they all do.

Disengage the clutch and try the starter in short **cold start** bursts, with a few minutes interval after three minutes to avoid flooding the carburettor. With a well charged battery, the right grade of oil, good spark plugs and a properly adjusted ignition you can count on getting your car started at -10 °C, even after a night or two in the open. But below that temperature, your engine may need a bit of encouragement from some boosting mixture that you spray into the carburettor. If you don't have such a spray, just pour a couple of kettles of boiling water over the engine exhaust manifold and try again with your starter.

The power of your battery is so essential that it's a good thing to carry a pair of jump leads that enable you to connect it to somebody else's battery while starting. With these you can also help a neighbour whose car won't start.

Failing any of these facilities, you may have to ask for a tow. Taxi drivers will sometimes oblige, although they aren't supposed to. The best bet is the smaller type of truck or van. Just stand by the road with your tow rope and have a rouble or two handy to compensate the driver for his time. He may refuse them, but have them ready just the same.

If there has been a thaw followed by a hard frost, you may find your door locks jammed. One trick (if you can get the key into the lock) is to heat the key with your cigarette lighter, then leave it in the lock for a minute. Repeat several times. But the best thing is to spray the lock with anti-freeze mixture beforehand. The spray sold in Russian shops has an attachment for insertion into the keyhole. Such things need to be bought before the frosts start. The Russians have a saying, 'If you want to ride in winter, buy your sledge in summer.' It has wide applications.

One of the commonest faults that cars develop

in damp weather is oxidising of the battery terminals. If you are the kind of driver who doesn't often look under the engine cover, this is the first thing you should check when your car stops for no apparent reason. It's easily remedied as long as you have a spanner to detach the leads and something to scrape them with. Smear the terminals and clamps with Vaseline (petroleum jelly) to prevent a recurrence.

winter driving
The biggest contribution you can make to your own and other people's safety in winter is to invest in snow tyres, at least for your rear wheels. The Scandinavian type with a heavy tread and metal studs is the best. They are sold in the Beryozka shops, through the Diplomatic Corps Service Bureau (UPDK), and some garages catering for foreigners have them.

Main roads in cities and between cities are cleared regularly in winter but there is no guarantee against sudden snowstorms, the thaw that often follows, and the subsequent freeze-up. And besides main roads, there are plenty of side lanes, yards and parking places where snow and ice accumulate, and without tyres that grip you can get embarassingly stuck. Another must is a handy-sized spade, for clearing snow from under your wheels. Snow under the frost is often the reason for the rear wheels turning ineffectively.

Chains are inconvenient and rarely used. There are no restrictions on the use of studded tyres, but wise people put a notice 'studs' (ШИПЫ) or a sign (Ⅰ) in their rear window to warn you of their increased stopping power. Most of the minor accidents in winter occur when a driver is unable to stop quickly enough to prevent himself sliding into the car in front. So keep a reasonable distance between your car and the one ahead, particularly when approaching junctions. And another point to remember: if you stop suddenly but with room to spare, at once let your car roll forward gently to give the person behind an extra chance.

If you do go into a skid, the rule is — front wheel skid: feet off, straighten front wheels until control restored; rear wheel skid: both feet off as before, turn into skid momentarily, then steer out of it. To avoid skidding, pump the brake pedal gently rather than jam your foot down hard.

parking

The international no-stopping and no-parking signs are used everywhere, and there are plenty of traffic police to pick you up for ignoring them. As more and more cars come on the road, the number of these signs has increased. But as yet, you can usually find a parking place not too far from your destination without much trouble. Give archways and tram- and bus-stops a wide berth. And for the sake of your car don't park just behind a stationary truck, whose driver may not notice your presence.

winter rule

In winter there are fewer private cars on the road, but there may be a lot of snow. The snow clearance service sweeps it into large roadside heaps at intervals of about fifteen metres. You are allowed to park between these heaps, but only when they are not about to be scooped up into lorries and driven away. In Moscow the even-numbered side of the street is cleared on the odd days of the month, so on odd days you must park on the odd side, and vice versa.

Moscow is just getting its first multi-storey garage. Garage space is hard to come by and, for foreigners, expensive. This probably means that your car will spend most of its time in the open, which is a fact that should make you think twice about buying a very smart type of vehicle. However, Russians claim that driving a car out of the cold into a heated garage and the condensation this causes is the best way of ensuring that your car rusts to pieces in a few years.

All this should not deter you from driving in winter. The air is usually dry and cold, fog is unusual, and your car is invaluable for getting you out to places where you can enjoy pastimes like cross-country skiing, or just for getting you about in comfort.

theft Always lock your car when you leave it. Not that a car with foreign number plates is likely to be stolen, but pilfering of radios, spare tyres and so on is not uncommon. Russian drivers always take off their windscreen wipers and lock them up with the car. If yours are easily removable, you should do the same. Snow tyres complete with the wheels are another common target. Consult a Russian mechanic on how to foil the tyre thief. He will probably offer you a wheel nut or bolt that requires a special shape of wrench. Some foreign car firms, such as Volvo, also supply theft-proof wheel nuts.

accidents To be able to claim insurance, you must have the circumstances of the accident registered by the traffic police. Even if you don't intend making a claim, you will need a certificate from them in order to get the damage repaired Service stations will insist on this, unless the damage is very slight. It is generally accepted, for instance, that a cracked windscreen is nobody's fault.

If you are touring, the formalities will be taken care of by Intourist, but remember the following.

Whatever the circumstances of the accident, you should try to get a traffic patrolman on the scene as soon as possible. If someone has been injured, he will call an ambulance and organise any other assistance that may be needed. The roads on Intourist itineraries are fairly well patrolled, but if you are a long way from anywhere, you may have to stop a passing car or truck and ask for help (*pómoshch*).

In any case, you will need the patrolman's report as the first step towards claiming insurance. The next step is to ask the Intourist office to arrange the rest.

If you are not a tourist and the accident occurs when you are driving about town, you should also contact the traffic police, by phone if necessary (no coins needed, just dial 02). The patrolman will write a report of the accident and in a day or two you will be able to collect a certificate from his local office to take to the central GAI office (Prospekt Mira, 15) and obtain another certificate, which will enable you to get repairs done at a service station and to collect your insurance compensation. Check by phone (221 93 60) on when the office receives foreign motorists.

If your car has been damaged in some way while it was parked, the first thing to do before moving the car is to get a patrolman on the spot and show him the damage. Of course, if you don't want to claim insurance and intend to do your own repairs (an embassy garage will sometimes oblige), you may be able to skip these procedures.

accessories and spare parts

The Soviet highway code requires that you have a first-aid kit, prominently displayed, a fire extinguisher, and a warning triangle. If you have to stop to change a wheel, don't forget to use the triangle.

On a long trip, even if your car is in very good fettle, you should carry a few essential spares, such as spark plugs, contact points, and a fan belt. You won't be able to buy such items for British or American cars in the USSR, although for Volvos, Mercedes Benz, Fiat and a few other makes there are special service facilities in Moscow.

Some British firms, like Sealink, for instance, offer spare-part kits for hire. A plastic windscreen is a good thing to have with you in case a stone from a freshly gravelled road flies your way.

Russian mechanics, especially in out-of-the-way places, are ingenious when it comes to making do. On one trip, when I was stuck in the steppes with a faulty generator, a friendly ex-sailor made me a new bushing out of a brass tap. It's a good thing to have a few souvenirs with which to show your gratitude on such occasions.

owning a car

Only members of diplomatic and other missions, correspondents, and representatives of foreign firms and banks who are registered with the Ministry for Foreign Affairs are allowed to import cars. No duty is charged, provided the importer undertakes to take the car out of the country when he or she leaves. There is an exception to this rule for diplomats, who are allowed to sell their cars to other foreigners without exporting or paying duty.

Lesser mortals have to export their cars, and once a car is exported from the USSR it cannot be reimported. The old ruse for selling your unwanted vehicle to another member of the foreign community by conducting the deal in Helsinki no longer works. This does not mean, of course, that you can't drive out to Finland or wherever and drive in again if you are still resident in the USSR.

Foreigners who are not registered with the Ministry for Foreign Affairs — e.g., students, or foreign employees of Soviet firms — are not normally allowed to import cars, but they can buy Soviet makes for hard currency. There are one or two advantages to running a Soviet car in the USSR, the main one being that you don't have to pay so much for repairs and spare parts, on which there is a heavy import duty.

To compete with the foreign market, the Russians offer their own makes (Volga, Lada, Niva, Moskvitch) at prices well below the cost of their Western counterparts. The latest Lada, for instance, though not very sophisticated, is a handy compact model. The Niva is a four-wheel drive cross-country vehicle resembling the Landrover, but lighter and less expensive. The Volga is a roomy limousine and can also be bought in the estate car version.

Foreigners pay no road tax. But you must have *no tax* your car registered and obtain Soviet licence plates, which currently cost about 25 roubles. This is done through an organisation known as GAI, short for *Gosavtoinspektsiya*, the state vehicle inspection authority. If you are registered with the Ministry, you do this through the Diplomatic Corps Service Bureau (UPDK), which also registers your car and gives you a letter to take to the GAI office, where your

vehicle is inspected (it must have even at this
stage a first-aid kit, warning triangle and fire-
extinguisher) and collect your licence plates.
There are different kinds of licence plates for
different kinds of foreigners. At present
diplomats have a light-red plate with a white
D. Employees of embassies who do not rank
as diplomats have a T instead of a D. Correspondents have yellow plates with a black K and
number, and business people yellow with a
black M and number. If you are not connected
with UPDK, you ask the foreign relations
department at your place of work to give
you a letter for GAI.

When your car has been registered, you are
given a card known as the *tekhtalón*, which
summarises the data on your car's technical
passport, kept at GAI. Keep this card with
your licence in case a traffic policeman wants
to see it.

A driving licence issued in the Soviet Union
has a removable card (*talón preduprezhdèniy*),
which a policeman can clip on the spot for
offences such as jumping the lights. Three
clips in a year means that you lose the card
and may have to take a test to get it back.

*import
procedure* Most people who decide to own a Western
make of car order it from a dealer in Helsinki
and sometimes go there to collect it themselves.
It's a long drive back but rather a pleasant one.
At the border there will be several formalities
to go through, including a close inspection of
the car, so leave Helsinki early in the day.

If you don't drive the car in, you or your
driver will have to go and pick it up at the
Butovo Customs House, 26 kilometres outside
Moscow on the Varshavskoye Highway (which
in spite of its name isn't the road to Warsaw).
It's rather a long way, so check up before you
go (tel. 541 79 97). A point to remember is

that all charges there have to be paid in hard currency.

In either case you will end up with a customs document saying you have brought the car into the country. This has to be submitted to the Central Moscow Customs House (Komsomolskaya Ploshchad, tel. 208 44 23) before you can go through the other formalities for obtaining licence plates.

renting a car

This has not yet been properly developed in the USSR, but car-hire facilities exist in quite a number of cities. If you are not fond of driving long distances, you may find it possible to hire a car at some point along your chosen route, where you would like to see more of the country. For instance, you may not want to cover the whole 4,000 kilometres of the Caucasus itinerary starting from Moscow. In this case the thing to do is to fly to, say, Tbilisi or Sochi, and hire a car there. You will be able to visit only the places on the Intourist itinerary, but those offer quite a lot of scope and probably the safest roads.

Self-drive hire facilities at present are available in Brest, Yerevan, Kiev, Kishinev, Leningrad, Lvov, Minsk, Moscow, Odessa, Sochi, Sukhumi, Tbilisi, Kharkov and Yalta.

In Batumi, Bukhara, Vilnius, Riga, Samarkand, Tallinn and Tashkent you have to have a chauffeur.

The initial charge for hiring a self-drive Lada car is rather low — currently 9.40 roubles per day. But mileage at 10 kopecks a kilometre quickly brings the price up to the Western level. There is also a 1.50 roubles per day charge for insurance, which covers you against damage to the car and third party but not against minor theft.

Since facilities are rather limited, you will have to ask Intourist to book you a car well in advance. In Moscow the only car-hire organisation is at the Ukraine Hotel (tel. 243 31 56) and you may have to wait ten days for a car. But advance bookings by cable are accepted.

seat belts   Since September 1984 the use of seat belts by the driver and front-seat passenger has been compulsory.

Food

Russians are fond of eating out but they don't do it very often. When they do, they make rather an occasion of it, spend a lot of money on food and drink, tip generously and take hours over their meal. This is what most of the best restaurants are geared to and the service operates accordingly, particularly in the evenings.

There is often a band and a space for dancing. With the coming of electronic amplification most of the music has become

quite deafening. If you are in the right mood and have strong eardrums, it can be jolly and you will have the chance of seeing how Russians enjoy themselves. But it's not the thing for a quiet chat over a meal.

To get this in the evening, you will have to rely, at least at first, on what Intourist or Beryozka offer for travellers from abroad. In any case act in advance, make your wishes clear and inquire about prices. Some of the select hard-currency restaurants are no less expensive than their Western counterparts.

Of course, this kind of thing is mainly for independent travellers. If you are with a group, you will have all the main meals laid on for you at the hotel where you are staying and will probably feel quite well fed. It would be a mistake to expect something very much different from an outside restaurant, except perhaps a famous Georgian or Azerbaijani establishment, such as the Aragvi or the Baku, where *shashlyk* (kebab) and *plov* (pilau) are the speciality. You probably wouldn't come to Moscow to visit a Chinese or Indian restaurant, although there are one or two of these in town.

going it alone

Anybody from abroad who lives in the USSR and has some knowledge of Russian will want to try a few experiments in eating out. If you refer to a Moscow telephone directory to find out what restaurants are available, a point to remember is that in recent years the restaurants in many of the larger hotels have gone 'residents only'. You may be able to get in by appealing to the manager (*administrátor*), but it's wise to inquire by telephone first. Ask for the name of whoever takes the order, if they book you a table.

Restaurants in the USSR never display their bill of fare and prices outside. Probably the reason for this is that prices are state-controlled and depend only on what category of restaurant the food is served in. So once you know what category the restaurant is, you can tell roughly how much you are going to pay for a *bef-stroganoff*, a plate of *borshch*, and so on. Some restaurants, even in the top category, offer a cheaper set meal during the day. If this is so, the times when the set meal is served will be displayed outside along with the restaurant's opening and closing times. A typical programme would be *à la carte* and set meals but no music from 11.30 a.m. to 4 p.m., then a break of a couple of hours, and then *à la carte* meals and music (starting about 8 p.m.) until 11.30 p.m.

All restaurants have cloakrooms, where you must leave your hat and coat. There are no racks or stands for them inside. You are not obliged to tip the attendants but most people do — about a rouble. You should also tip the doorman if he has been helpful. Waiters add a 10% cover charge. Check your bill if it looks too big — waiters do make mistakes sometimes. Tip 10% to 15% if the service has been satisfactory.

tipping

If you don't know the restaurant, don't go by the menu. Ask the waiter's advice about the main dish and take what he suggests, unless it runs right against your taste.

what to order

A Russian meal usually begins with *zakóoski* — starters. The commonest nowadays are some kind of smoked, salted or tinned fish, potato salad with chopped pickled gherkins and small pieces of meat or fish in it, and fresh cucumbers and tomatoes when in season. In a good restaurant you sometimes have a choice between various kinds of cured sturgeon. The main distinction is between raw (*hulódnoye*, cold) and cooked (*guryáchye*, hot) curing. There are three basic kinds of sturgeon. In descending order of their natural size they are the *belóoga*, the *sevróoga*, and the *osyótr*. The flesh of the *osyótr* (*osetréena*) is more delicate, and therefore more often cooked than cured. An even smaller variety, the *sterlyad*, or sterlet, is delicious but seldom obtainable.

'zakóoski'

There are several kinds of vegetable paste which, rather confusingly are known as 'ikra' (caviare), but have nothing to do with fish roe, the most common being made from egg-plant.

Proper caviare is not as plentiful as it used to be, but good restaurants have it and there are several different ways of eating it. It comes in three varieties: 'black granular' (*chórnaya zernístaya*), which is the best and most expensive, 'black pressed' (*páyusnaya*) and 'red caviare' (*kétovaya*), which is the eggs not of sturgeon but of the Quinnat salmon. The simplest way of eating caviare is to spread it on buttered toast or white bread, but the traditional Russian style is to have it with 'bleeny' — unsweetened pancakes. You spread the butter on the pancake, then the caviare, roll it all up, cut it to a suitable size and pop it in your mouth. Vodka is the obvious thing to drink with caviare, but if you have no taste for the national beverage, dry Georgian wines or champagne go down very well.

The usual thing if you go to a restaurant with friends is to order several different *zakóoski* and share them out. They may include cold ham and smoked sausage, and by the time you've got them all they begin to look like a meal in themselves.

soups   A full scale meal would include soup as well as starters, but often one replaces the other. Russian soups are very filling.

The best known soups are, of course, *shchee* (cabbage soup) and *borshch* (beetroot soup). In winter, *shchee* is always made with salted cabbage (a kind of sauerkraut) cooked in a meat broth. It should have pieces of stewed beef or pork in it and be served with *smetána* (soured cream). In summer, the Russians make a green *shchee*, with fresh cabbage. Green *shchee* should have several herbs sprinkled over it, such as fennel or parsley, and some chopped spring onions. This is, of course, better for your cholesterol level, but not half as tasty as the winter variety.

Borshch is similar to *shchee*, with the addition of sliced beetroot, which gives it its characteristic red colour and sweetish flavour. It should also have bacon, chopped meat and sausage in it, and be served with soured cream.

Properly prepared *shchee* and *borshch* are very good, but they vary in quality from day to day and at different times of the day because the vegetables and meat may become overcooked. So it is worth inquiring which soup is better at the time you are ordering. Incidentally, for those who eat at home, both these soups usually taste better on the second day, but they must, of course, be kept in a cold place.

'solyánka' and others

The main feature of *solyánka* is chopped salted cucumbers and olives. The soup is made out of boiled meat or fish, so you can order either a meat (*myasnáya*) or a fish (*ríbnaya*) *solyánka*. It is rather an uncertain quantity as the salted cucumbers tend to get the upper hand over the other ingredients. *Harchó* is another fairly common soup. Of Caucasian origin and made of mutton, it's usually rich and heavily spiced, particularly with garlic. A milder type of soup is *lapshá*, which means noodles. Actually the soup thus called is chicken broth with chicken and noodles in it.

second course

Russian steaks (*beefstéks*) are often of rather indifferent quality, the meat having been frozen. Russians make up for this by slicing them and serving them with a rich sauce — the well known *bef-stroganoff* — and by grinding them up for hamburgers. A *kutléta*, unless otherwise stated, is also a kind of 'burger' with something else besides meat in it. But a genuine Kiev *kutlèta* is chicken breast slices wrapped round a large piece of butter. You have to be careful, when you cut it open, that the butter doesn't spurt over you.

Sturgeon comes boiled, fried or spit-grilled (*na vertelyè*). If you want potatoes or other vegetables with your grill, you may have to order them. Otherwise the fish arrives looking rather forlorn, alone on the plate with only a few onions and cucumbers.

The other most notable speciality is the chicken *tabakà*, which is half a young chicken, spiced and fried. The Georgians and Armenians usually serve it with various herbs, such as *kinza* (coriander) leaves, which they claim will make you live to a hundred. *Kinza* certainly adds an interesting flavour besides the promise of longevity.

Shashlyk (kebab) and *tabakà* are usually treated as the culmination after a good round of starters or soup and are not usually eaten with anything except a sauce, onions and bread. Lettuce is something of a rarity in Russian restaurants, although young lettuce leaves (*salàt*) are widely sold at the market in summer.

smaller dishes   I have already mentioned *bleeny*, unsweetened pancakes. There is an important distinction between them and the *bleenchik*, which is also a pancake, but rolled up with meat, jam or cottage cheese inside, and browned in a frying pan. You can often have these as a third course or as a light second course.

Another famous Russian speciality that is eaten at all times is *piroshkèe*. This is often translated as pies, but in fact *piroshkèe* are more like unsweetened doughnuts, filled not with jam but with chopped meat or boiled cabbage. Some restaurants serve them with a clear soup. They are sold at stalls in the streets or at railway stations and are also available sometimes at another important food establishment, the *koolinarèeya* (prepared-food shop). *Piroshkèe* can also be made of flaky pastry (*sloyòneeye*).

The Caucasian variant of *piroshkèe* is *cheburèkee*, which are bigger, made out of unleavened dough and have a filling of spiced mutton. These are sold in Georgian and Armenian restaurants and at smaller establishments, known as *cheboorechnaya*, where you can either eat them on the spot or buy them to take home and warm up.

Another type of 'fast food' is the Russian *pelmènee*, a small meat dumpling, served hot with soured cream or butter. Originally a Siberian invention, made in quantity by the whole family and their guests and kept outside in the snow until wanted, they are nowadays sold frozen in packets and are very easily boiled up at home — or kept in the freezer till you need them. Don't buy them or use them unless they rattle in the packet, indicating they are still well frozen. If dressed up with salad or peppers, they make a quick and satisfying meal.

vegetables

Because of the short summer and long winter the Russians have a lot of trouble growing vegetables and storing them. Lettuces don't usually have hearts and are chopped up small with cream or mayonnaise. On the other hand, the cabbage tradition is highly developed. When Russians talk about cabbage (*kapbosta*), they usually mean the big white variety that matures in autumn. This kind stores well and can be shredded and salted down to make a standby all through the winter, providing an essential ingredient for soups, and also a side-dish dressed with salad oil to be eaten before or with a meal. There is a distinction between salted cabbage and pickled cabbage, which has vinegar in it and consequently far less vitamins. Russian housewives often express disapproval of vinegar. They would never think of putting it on beetroot, for instance, which is another important winter standby. Apart from using beetroot in *borshch*, the Russians slice it up with potatoes, salted gherkins, onions and carrots, making a salad known as *vinegrèt*, which is usually dressed with sunflower oil.

Forest mushrooms are almost a cult in central Russia and Siberia. People go out to gather them singly and in large parties, bring them home and peel them together, and spend the evening over frying pans full of their spoils. The mushrooms are cooked with onions and potatoes. Ceps (*byèliye*), chanterelles (*lesèechky*), brown caps (*pudberyòzoviky*) and orange caps (*pudosìnoviky*) are the best varieties. A good rule for the beginner is to avoid all others. You need some instruction and experience to distinguish between the poisonous and edible kinds, but if you can get a Russian to take you out in the woods on a mushroom-picking expedition, you can be assured of a pleasurable day and some good fellowship. The forest mushroom differs from the field or cultivated variety (known in Russian as 'champignon') in texture and taste, which is less pungent but more varied and subtle. If you can't gather them yourself, you can buy them in late summer or autumn at the market, where there are charts on the walls to guide you. Again stick to the main varieties.

Mushrooms are also salted down, usually with spice, herbs and sometimes garlic and vinegar. This is another culinary art, often practised by the master of the house, who proudly treats his guests to samples from his stock long after mushrooming days are over. Pickled mushrooms are, of course, another popular *zakóska*.

other wild foods

Russians are keen on, and can still gather in their forests, quite a few wild fruits. The seasons of wild strawberries, raspberries, bilberries, red whortleberries and cranberries are, of course, short, and you have to look out for them at the markets, where the prices are rather high. The cranberry is particularly important. It will keep all winter long in a refrigerator or out in the frost. Though rather tart, it makes a splendid jam or a sauce for meat or poultry. If you happen to be driving down from Leningrad in autumn and notice cranberries for sale by the roadside, it's well worth buying a pailful. Some of the wild berries find their way into the shops in the form of jams or other preserves.

An important shop in this sphere is the *lesnáya bil* where you can buy, according to season, quails, partridges, capercaillie, and even bear and elk steaks. The difficulty with the birds is that you may have to pluck them at home, which is a messy job in a flat. But for a small extra charge some shops will prepare them for you, if you order them a day in advance.

Lesnáya bil shops also sell honey, and pollen sugar, a powerful stimulant. You can also buy various types of honey at market, often in the comb.

cereals

The Soviet food industry is a long way behind in the production of packaged breakfast cereals. Ordinary cornflakes and wheatflakes appeared for a few years but now seem to have been withdrawn from production. Other varieties are unknown. If you rely on packaged cereals this leaves you with a breakfast problem, unless you can import from Finland or have access to an embassy commissariat.

One solution is to go over to the traditional Russian cereals — buckwheat, semolina, and oatmeal porridge. Oatmeal (*gerkoolès*, i.e., Hercules) is the same as ours, though not 'instant', and semolina goes down well with raisins or stewed dried fruit (dried fruit for stewing is a common Russian dessert, sold at most greengrocers and known as *kompòt*).

Buckwheat, if you can find it in the shops, is well worth trying. Rich in iron and rutin, it is probably the least processed of all grain cereals. You wash the grain, then tip it into a saucepan of boiling water with salt and let the water boil away slowly, taking off any scum with a spoon. When the grain is soft and *all* the water has boiled away, you take the saucepan off the gas, wrap it up in a towel and leave it for an hour or two (some Russians put it under a pillow). The result is the traditional *kasha* of Russian folk-tale and has been in use for centuries. There is an art in getting the proper proportion of water and grain, so that the grain cooks to the right consistency in its own steam. Two cups of water to one of buckwheat is about right.

You will probably find it easier to buy your first *kasha* ready cooked at one of the prepared-food shops, preferably when it's still warm. You can eat it if for breakfast with milk (don't forget to add some salt) and with meat and sauce for your main meal. *Kàsha* keeps well in a cool place for two or even three days.

buckwheat, American style   An American health food enthusiast, who became very keen on buckwheat, told me he ate it raw. He kept it moist in a saucer until it sprouted, then ate it like mustard and cress.

The other staple breakfast food for Russians is **milk**
milk in various forms. The Russians call
yoghourt *prostokvásha* and they have several
other types of fermented milk besides, the
most popular being *kefîr*. All of them are
supposed to be better for the stomach than
ordinary whole milk.

Russians are also very fond of that forgotten
food cottage cheese, which they call *tvórog*.
This is sold in the shops with various fat
contents and sometimes in the form of a paste,
but a lot of people make it themselves by
straining milk that has been left to turn and
then warmed up, through a piece of cheesecloth.
Besides eating it with sugar or *kefîr*, they put it
in dumplings and fry it in fritters (with an
egg added). It is also the main ingredient in the
paskha with which Orthodox Christians break
their fast on Easter Sunday. *Paskha* has a lot
of other things in it besides, including candied
peel, raisins and eggs, and is eaten with a light
cake known as a *kooléech*. You may notice
these at the bakers' shops around Easter time
by their characteristically tall round shape.
Nowadays they are usually called 'spring
cakes'.

One thing that the milk marketing people
do with milk may not be to everybody's taste.
To solve the problem of storage, they sell
quite a lot of milk that has been reconstituted
(i.e., made up from powder) as ordinary milk.
It tastes almost the same as ordinary milk and
is only really noticeable in tea, which Russians
don't often drink with milk. But foreigners,
English tea-drinkers for example, may take
exception. Soviet reconstituted milk seems to
behave in exactly the same way as ordinary
pasteurised milk when it comes to making
yoghourt or cottage cheese, so it can't be
too far removed from the natural product.

The same cannot be said for 'longlife' milk,

which gets just as nasty in old age as its English counterpart. A much nicer-tasting but rather rare variety is Mozhaisk milk. With a flavour something like 'Ideal' milk it is excellent in coffee. Funnily enough, it is never labelled and can be identified only by its bottle — like an ordinary lemonade bottle with a metal cap but a longer neck.

cooking for one

If you are looking after yourself or want to avoid too much bother in the kitchen, you should find a good *koolinaríya* (prepared-food shop). They vary in the quality and variety of their offerings. Their meat will sometimes be a problem, unless you are an expert cook, but their hamburgers are usually quite acceptable. The good *koolinaríya* should have prepared chickens, stuffed duck, fried fish, which Russians often eat cold, salads and pastry. The best in Moscow is probably the one under the Prague Restaurant, top of Arbat Street.

eggs and bacon

For some reason Russian shops (except Beryozka) never sell bacon rashers nowadays, but they do sometimes have large sides of bacon. If you're fond of eggs and bacon, scout around till you spot one of these and, if it's pink and not too fat, ask them to cut you off half a kilo, then learn to slice it up yourself with a bread knife.

Incidentally, if you order fried eggs (*yaèechnitsa*) in a cafe or restaurant, you always get at least two, in a small metal frying pan, which is sometimes very hot. Unless you say you want it 'naturálnaya', it may come as a kind of omelette, especially if you asked for ham (*vetchiná*) with it. Boiled eggs are usually hard-boiled, unless you say *vsmyàtku* (soft-boiled) or *v meshòchek* (medium).

The main cooking oil is made from sunflower **oil**
seeds, and Russians also use it as a salad
dressing. At first you may not like its nutty
smell and flavour. Corn (maize) oil is sometimes
available and imported olive oil is sold for hard
currency. Margarine made largely of vegetable
oil is always to be had and rather cheap.

Fish and chips, the 'great British invention', **fish**
has not yet reached the Soviet Union, but
Russians do eat a lot of fish, apart from the
famous sturgeon. Much fish is frozen and
packaged, especially that sold at the big fish
stores known as *Okeàn* (Ocean). It's easier
and safer for the inexperienced to buy frozen
fish. The commonest are cod (*treskà*), hake
(*hek*), *ledyannàya* and *mintài*, all good sea
fish for frying.

There are many kinds of salted, smoked and
otherwise cured fish, particularly the herring.
All are appreciated by Russian beer- and vodka-
drinkers. But the one that really sends them is
the *vòbla*, the dried Caspian roach. It's as
popular as kippers in England or crabs in
Baltimore, and eaten in the same way as in
that city — off a newspaper.

The USSR is the world's biggest wheat grower **bread**
and most Russians eat quite a lot of bread
(*hleb*) — it's cheap and they believe it's good
for them. The kind they eat most of probably
is. The famous 'black' (*chòrny*) is not really
black, although it does have an almost black
crust on top, with a slightly bitter taste much
valued by the connoisseurs, especially vodka-
drinkers. Made of rye, it has plenty of vitamins
and less starch and fats than the white breads,
so it's a good thing to eat if you want to keep
your weight down. Don't confuse *chòrny* with
borodìnsky, a delicious dark sweet bread,

recognisable by the caraway seeds on top. And don't eat too much of either — they overtax some people's stomachs.

Two other browns are worth remembering — *ukráinsky* (Ukrainian) and *stolóvy* (table). The wheat flour added to the rye makes them lighter in both colour and texture.

Ordinary bread shops nowadays are nearly all self-service. The loaves and buns are piled on shelves and you select what you want and walk along to the cash-desk to pay for it. You will notice some long-handled spoons lying on the edge of the shelf. These are for testing the bread, to see if it's fresh and soft — you're not supposed to touch it and, once you have, you shouldn't put it back.

Different shops get their deliveries at different times, some quite late in the afternoon, to supply the flow of customers coming home from work. The quality of the breads varies and it's worth shopping around to find out which bakers have the best, and when. In Moscow the best baker's is considered to be the one next to Gastronom No. 1 in Gorky Street. People still call it Filipoff's, after its former owner.

Some bakers have a much bigger selection than others, including some health breads. A *boolochnaya* that sells cakes and sweets as well as bread is called a *boolochnaya-kondeeterskaya*, and a shop that sells just cakes and sweets is a *kondeeterskaya*.

Russians have sweets similar to ours, although they favour strong plain chocolate rather than milk. Their boxes of chocolates come in several different shapes and sizes, but are basically of two kinds — *assortée* and *nabór*. A *nabór* contains chocolates with several different centres, but in an *assortée* all the centres are the same though the shapes may differ.

Incidentally, when the Russians talk about a *tort*, they mean not a tart but a fancy cake. And when they say 'cakes' (*keks*), they mean 'a fruit cake'.

Drink

tea and the samovar The days of the traditional samovar are probably numbered. Modern Russians use electric ones or kettles, and don't appear to drink the enormous quantities of tea that their ancestors are said to have done. But the old samovar is by no means extinct. It made a comeback recently as a collector's item and many families still have one tucked away somewhere that they take with them to their *dácha* (country cottage) in summer.

Tea with a samovar on the veranda is a charming custom. The preliminaries are as follows. The samovar is taken out into the garden and filled with water, probably from a well or pump. The chimney is then packed with pine-tree cones, which are lighted at the bottom with splinters of pine. The water boils quickly and, when all the cones have burnt away, the samovar is carried indoors and placed on a special tray, so that no ash or hot water falls on the tablecloth. A little stand is fitted on top of the chimney to hold the teapot, which is steadily replenished with hot water from the tap at the bottom of the samovar. The combination of well water and pine smoke usually produces a good brew.

tea and jam Russians seldom drink tea with milk and, compared with the British, take it rather weak. They make up for this by drinking it with lemon (*leemón*) or with jam (*varénye*), for which each person has a small side dish (*rozétka*). There is an important distinction between *varénye* and what the Russians call *dzhem* (from our 'jam'). Actually it's the same as our distinction between 'home-made' and 'shop' jam respectively, except that *varènye* is sold in shops and Russians often put a spoonful or two into their tea. They used rather unjustly to associate our jam with their *poveèdlo*, which has no whole fruit in it at all. However, imports of Western-style jams from Bulgaria, Poland and Hungary are gradually getting things into perspective.

In places where the water supply is suspect, a samovar comes in useful because, even after you have finished tea drinking, it leaves you with an ample supply of safe drinking water. If you drink tea without milk, you will gradually become aware of the different taste of the water in different places. This is something Russians often comment on. The best water for tea-making I ever experienced was in Samarkand, where they drink mostly green tea. But when travelling about it's better not to drink straight from any tap. Moscow water is generally considered to be very good, but the taps of Leningrad, a city built on a marsh and with a huge system of ancient canals, are not to be relied on.

water supply

However, Soviet shops and restaurants and cafès can often offer you one or two kinds of bottled mineral water from the country's numerous spas. They vary from being pleasantly tasteless to having a taste that you will only put up with if you want to cure the troubles that the label on the bottle tells you, in minute letters, they are good for. *Narzàn, Moskòvskaya* and *Slavyànskaya* are pleasant table waters and a good substitute for soda water in drinks.

mineral waters

The curative ones, like *Borzhomi*, need to be taken regularly, at special times and the right temperature to be effective. And of course you need to know which one to take for your particular ailment.

vodka   Having mentioned tea, we should pass on to the other national beverage. Vodka is now so well known in the West as an ingredient in cocktails that it hardly requires any introduction. But the Russian habit of drinking it straight and usually with something to eat probably does need our attention. If you offer a Russian vodka, you must also offer some kind of open sandwich. At a pinch our little cocktail biscuits will do (because of the novelty), but it's far better to prepare something more substantial, like salami, herrings or other salted fish, gherkins, and so on.

The best kinds of vodka are *stolíchnaya, psheníchnaya*, (distilled from wheat), *Sibírskaya*, and *Moskóvskaya Osóbaya*. Other, cheaper kinds are made from inferior materials, not so thoroughly refined, and more likely to have after effects. Formerly, in homes where vodka was drunk, a small decanter stood on the sideboard among the wine glasses. If a friend called and would have a drink, the glasses and the decanter came down from the sideboard on to the table, a plate of sandwiches appeared and the drinking went on at the table. Nowadays the vodka is kept in the fridge.

In polite company, vodka is usually drunk from smallish wine glasses. Of course, when men get together, it may be drunk from anything, but rarely just the bottle. During the war it was drunk from a mess tin with any medals that had recently been won submerged in it.

The rather old joke (*anekdót*) is told of Agent 03, who had not been briefed properly before being spirited into the country. When he reached the nearest village two men came up on either side of him and said, 'You'll be

number three'. The agent put his hands up,
but all his 'captors' had been looking for was
a third person with whom to split the cost and
contents of a half-litre bottle.

There may be times when you don't want to
drink. Among Russians there are three valid
excuses for not doing so, apart from natural
reasons of ill health, such as blood pressure,
ulcers, and so on. The first is that you have to

opting out

drive (but nobody goes to a party in their own
car), the second is that you have to work that
evening or early next morning, and the third
is that you have a date with a girl friend. So if
you don't like drinking, it's a good thing to have
a lot of work to do or a lot of girl friends. All
other things being equal, most Russian women
will be delighted to meet a man who doesn't
drink.

Note: in a recent move against alcoholism, the
legal age for purchasing alcoholic drinks was
raised from 21 and shops were prohibited from
selling them before 2 p.m. Intourist establishments, however, will function as usual.

If you do happen to have had too much to
drink, various traditional cures for the hangover
are recommended. One is the brine from salted
cucumbers, another is a special soup, *khàshi*,

hangovers

made from mutton bones and entrails, but the
simplest is to take 'a hair of the dog that bit
you', i.e., another nip of vodka. If you can
face it, it's quite effective. Usage has given the
Russians just one word for this. Unfortunately
it has five syllables and may prove a bit of
a tongue-twister on the morning after —
opokhmeleetsya. An aspirin (*aspireen*) may be
just as good.

wines Rather surprisingly, considering their taste for
vodka, most Russians prefer sweet wines to dry.
Russian women certainly do. Many of these
wines, of the Port or Madeira type, come from
the Crimea.

Most of the dry wines are made in the
Caucasus. Georgian wines are named after the
kind of grape, or the district in which it is
grown, but they are also numbered from 1—30
in order of sugar content, *Tsinandali*, No. 1, a
white wine, having the smallest.

Other good wines are produced in Moldavia
and in Central Asia. But to sample the latter
you have to go there, as they are not often
exported. Hungarian and Bulgarian wines,
Cuban rum and some Algerian wines are often
available in Moscow. Any details of what year
was good, however, seem to be a state secret.

bars The theory that you should always eat as well
as drink has resulted in there being not many
places where you can just drink in comfort.
Intourist has recognised this specific need of
the foreign tourist and opened hard-currency
bars in its main hotels. In recent years Moscow
has acquired quite a few vodka bars (*ryumoch-
naya*), where you have to buy a sandwich with
your drink, and several small café-bars with
soft lighting and not-so-soft music, which
serve a cocktail or two and seem to be very
popular with young people.

The Russians drink quite a lot of beer (*peevo*), and beer halls, which open at 10 a.m., are usually crowded. But there are not many of them and they seem to be furnished to discourage drinking, which some people may think is a good idea, although they don't. The choice of beers is small and shops and restaurants are often sold out. The beers most commonly found in Moscow are *Zhigulyovskoye*, a mild light ale, and *Moskovskoye*, slightly darker and stronger. *Leningradskoye* is twice as strong. Beers are usually sold in bottles, or on draught, in the beer halls, but recently a much stronger, canned beer *Zolotoye Koltso* (12% AC) has appeared in the better bars. Hard-currency shops stock Heinecker, and several other Western beers.

beer

All Soviet alcoholic drinks have the percentage of alcohol indicated on the bottle label. This should not be confused with British or US proof, the figures of which are usually much higher for an equivalent strength. Thus *stolichnaya* vodka (considered the best) is stated to have an alcohol content of 40%, which is equivalent to 70° British proof and 80% US proof. Many of the republics have formidable arrays of brandies, liqueurs and 'balsams' of similar or even greater strength. Their kick comes more slowly but no less forcefully.

proof and percentage

Kvass, a yeasty, non-alcoholic beer, is the traditional Russian thirst-quencher. It is usually sold in summer in the streets from large tanks and you can buy a half-litre mug for a few kopecks, or any quantity to take away with you, if you have a wide-necked can with a lid.

    During the Olympics a net of Pepsi-Cola stalls was spread across Moscow and they still function somewhat irregularly in summer. Slot-machine soda fountains, much cheaper,

thirst-quenchers

are quite common. And the Russians have also developed a Cola-type drink of their own, *Baikal*, which is not quite so sweet as Pepsi and is flavoured with stimulating Siberian herbs.

Western drinks   Western drinks are rather popular as a novelty. Russians are always eager to try whisky but sometimes disappointed by the taste. The habit of diluting it with water puzzles them and they usually prefer it neat. But a proper 'Scotch on the rocks' will have its appeal. Gin goes down very well, especially with tonic, and sloe gin never fails to please.

no drinks before dinner   As one might expect from what has been said already, Russians do not usually drink before a meal, although if you offer them a Western-style drink before dinner they will, of course, accept. The usual thing in a Russian home, after the kissing, hugging and handshakes are over, is for your host to show you whatever he wants to show you and then invite you straight to the table. There will probably be a good many bottles on it — wine, vodka, and possibly brandy (often contributed by the guests themselves). Russians often drink brandy, like vodka, at the start of a meal. This hardly does justice to the excellent Armenian and Georgian brandies on offer, but they seem to enjoy it.

toasts   Even when only a few friends are gathered together, there is nearly always some kind of toast before anyone starts drinking. The host usually proposes the first one.

On more important occasions a *tamadà* (toastmaster) is appointed and quite long speeches are made, especially in Georgia, where bucolic rites are strictly observed. Besides proposing toasts himself, the *tamadà* invites his guests to make them. As a foreign guest you are sure to be asked, so it's a good thing to be prepared. Russians are receptive to what is told them at first hand about other countries and customs and there's no need to be bashful about holding forth; but if you are shy, just toast your hosts and say how glad you are to be with them. This too will be much appreciated.

Unless you have somebody to act as interpreter, lack of language may prevent you from saying all you want to say. An English friend of mine, who had some red carpet treatment on a business trip, found a way round this. He wrote out his speech in advance, had it translated into Russian and then transliterated, i.e., written out more or less phonetically in the Latin alphabet. He then spoke it himself, albeit with an atrocious accent. The effect was hilarious and culminated in an ovation. But how many vodkas preceded the performance, I couldn't say.

Getting Down to Business

No one would think of entering into trade negotiations with a Soviet organisation without a good deal of previous consideration and preparation. In fact, many business people would probably say it is such a specialised field that the venture is hardly worth making.

political aspect A common assumption is that politics plays a decisive role. But this is true only in the very broad sense. The fact remains that while political relations with the West have been at an all-time low, Soviet trade with the industrially developed Western countries has risen from 1.5 billion (US 1500 billion) roubles in 1980, to about 4 billion (US 4000 billion) roubles in 1984.

organisation But that said, one has to admit that Soviet trade is organised in a very different way from that of the Western market economies. Its principle organisations, in order of importance, are the following:

> The Ministry of Foreign Trade
> The Foreign Trading Corporations
> The Soviet Trade Delegations abroad
> The Chamber of Commerce and Industry
> of the USSR
> The USSR Bank for Foreign Trade and
> the Moscow Narodny Bank in London
> Ingosstrakh (Insurance)
> Sovincentr (services to foreign business people)

corporations The ministry exercises overall control. The corporations and their representatives in the trade delegations negotiate and sign contracts, each in a specialised field, and are responsible to the ministry. Altogether there are about 80 of these corporations, known in Russian as *vsesoyuzniye obyedineniya*, or V/O for short. Their titles are slightly confusing. Very often they end in the word 'export', although the corporation in question may be almost as much concerned with importing as with exporting. V/O AVTOEXPORT, for instance, *exports and imports* all kinds of road transport vehicles and garage equipment. V/O EXPORTLYON, as its name suggests, exports flax (*lyon*), and many other natural fibres, but also *imports* wool, woollen fabrics and much else. V/O MACHINOEXPORT, however, only exports machinery because it has a sister corporation V/O MACHINOIMPORT, which only imports.

first approach

The corporations and their representatives in the various Soviet trade delegations abroad are the main targets for anyone who wants to sell goods to the Soviet Union. Your letters to them can be in English. They should contain as much technical information as possible and be sent with several copies, which may be passed on to prospective customers in the Soviet Union — industrial ministries, factories, scientific committees, and so on. If you know of such an organisation that has a specific need for your product, it is possible and useful to write to them directly at the same time. But how do you find out?

obtaining information

Much useful preliminary information can be gleaned at the Department of Trade in London and particularly its Statistic and Market Intelligence Library. (For the addresses and telephone numbers of these and other mentioned organisations, see the lists at the end of this book.) If you are visiting Moscow, it is also well worth calling at the Commercial Department of the British Embassy who have the offical statistics at their fingertips and are ready to advise on how and which Soviet organisations to approach. One of the things they will advise you to do is to copy to them any letters you write to Soviet organisations so that they can follow up the inquiry for you if, as quite often happens, there has been no response.

Two other important sources of information and advice are the British–Soviet Chamber of Commerce and the East European Trade Council in London. The former organises visits to the USSR for British business people, as do other, regional chambers of commerce in Britain. Business people from the United States should contact the US–USSR Trade and Economic Council.

advertising   Advertising of consumer goods just doesn't come into it. The Soviet authorities know very well that any good-quality Western product will quickly be bought up by the Soviet public — for the novelty, if for nothing else. Recent years have seen an increase in the amount of hard currency allocated for consumer goods but the overriding demand is still for capital goods and technologies that enable the country to go ahead with its huge overall development plans. They are used for stopping gaps and making up lags in various sectors of domestic production, and also as a means of stimulating the general level of productivity. The USSR is mainly interested in obtaining things it can't get from other countries in the Eastern bloc, i.e., such raw materials as natural rubber, wool, tin and in some years, wheat, butter and meat — not only when there is a bad harvest in the USSR but also when world prices are low. It also needs high technology for the petrochemical and energy-related industries. But this outline is so general that it hardly accounts for the huge success of the Fiat car deal, which gave birth to the Soviet Lada, of which there are now millions on Soviet roads and elsewhere, or for the Rank Xerox breakthrough in the field of copying machines more than a decade ago.

Very careful study is needed to foresee these trends. The Soviet economy is undeniably the most planned economy in the world but from time to time it displays some very spontaneous impulses. I remember a conversation I once had with the chairman of the State Committee for Science and Technology. He agreed with all my remarks about the pernicious anti-environmental nature of the private car, but confessed that Soviet planners had been unable to do without it as a stimulus to productivity and technological advance.

A lot can be done to bring your product to the notice of the people who matter in factories, committees, ministries and the boards of industries by advertising in Soviet technical journals. This is the monopoly of yet another V/O — the V/O Vneshtorgreklama, which will quote you a price for inserting advertisements in Soviet technical publications. The advertisements should be presented in such a way that factory managers or anyone else who may want to place an order can quote the essential specifications to higher authority.

A British company, British Industrial Publicity Overseas Ltd (Walter House, Bedford Street, WC2), puts out a Russian-language journal *Británskaya Promýshlennost i Tèkhnika* (British Industry and Engineering), which has regular and wide distribution among factories, institutes and specialists in the USSR. It also publishes an annual Directory of British Firms interested in Trade with the USSR, which reaches 'end-users' in the Soviet Union.

trade delegations to the USSR

One of the best ways of getting to know about trade prospects in Russia is to join a trade delegation from one of the regional chambers of commerce in the UK. Any appointments the members of the delegation have asked for are arranged to take place during the visit. In other words, the ministries and departments concerned set aside time and attention that might not be available for the individual business person. A delegation may also provide an opportunity of making contact with the 'end-user' of your product whose request or favourable opinion carries weight with the trading organisations.

No one claims that a lot will emerge from a first visit, but patience and persistence are key words in developing business with the Russians.

exhibitions

Yet another method of getting your product known to prospective Soviet customers is participation in Soviet exhibitions. By doing so you pick up several advantages. For one thing the exhibition programme (available from the Department of Trade) incorporates suggestions from the Soviet industrial ministries and is coordinated with the Foreign Trade Plan. The goods to be exhibited are approved by the Soviet authorities as being of interest to Soviet specialists, so there may be a chance of making sales from the stand. And, above all, an exhibition offers an opportunity of making contact with the people — factory managers, specialists and officials — who may start the ministerial wheels turning towards your product. It also gives you a chance of finding out what conditions the machinery or whatever you are selling may have to operate under. This is important when it comes to giving guarantees.

One consequence of the whole Soviet economy **negotiations** being geared to five-year and annual plans is that there are times of the year when the Foreign Trading Corporations know more about their future potential than at others. The work on annual plans is usually completed in October, and by November the corporations know what hard-currency allocations they have been granted and what they will be authorised to buy. It seems to be generally agreed that November to March is a favourable time for concluding contracts. Of course, a lot of preliminary work will have to be done before then and an agreement may be concluded earlier, but the final stroke is more likely to be added in this period.

In the early stages business people visiting Moscow for negotiations should allow themselves about three times longer than they would for similar talks in London, Paris or New York. The effort needed from the Westerner in this period is likely to be greater than that required in other parts of the world. On the other hand, once the business has been established and a routine worked out, its continuation and development may be a far less strenuous process than elsewhere.

Soviet trading organisations have the reputation **credit** of being good payers and very tough, well informed negotiators. Even without a credit agreement between the countries, credit is always available for deals with a buyer who has never been known to default. The only trouble is that, at present, interest rates are high and tend to put up the price of British goods. Various ways out of this difficulty have been proposed (such as invoicing in West German marks), but none has proved satisfactory to both sides.

guarantees   Guarantees (warranties) are another problem for the Western trader who may have very little idea of the conditions under which the product is to be used. It's important to make all the necessary provisos clear at an early stage.

interpreters   Interpreters are often provided by the Soviet corporations concerned. They are usually well versed in their subject but English idiom may sometimes defeat them. Most interpreters are reluctant to admit not having understood something you say and may try to guess their way out. If you notice any signs of hesitation, you should go slowly and avoid tricky expressions such as 'We must do some more homework on that' or 'Better go back to square one'. Although square one is exactly where you should go back to if you find your negotiating partner swinging off at a tangent.

This chapter only begins to scratch the surface of a complex and fascinating field. It is also oriented on Britain but the principles outlined here should apply to beginners in the Soviet market from other English-speaking and Third World countries. Although foreign trade is only a fraction of the Soviet Union's total economic activity, its trade turnover world wide has risen from 9 billion (US 9000 billion) roubles in 1980 to 14 billion (US 14000 billion) roubles in 1984 and is likely to go on rising.

public holidays   One final point to remember. Public holidays in the USSR are celebrated on the following days:

New Year's Day	1 January
International Women's Day	8 March
May Day	1 and 2 May
Victory Day	9 May
Constitution Day	7 October

October Revolution Day	7 and 8 *November*
	(not October)

If the holiday falls on a Tuesday, it is customary to declare Monday a holiday and work on the previous Saturday. Since celebrations in offices usually begin on the eve of the holiday the period from 30 April to 10 May is definitely not a good time for business visits.

Most offices work from 9 a.m. to 6 p.m. with a lunch break from 1 to 2 p.m. But some departments, such as Accounts, may begin an hour earlier and close at five.

Sport and Entertainment

no cricket In one respect, at least, Russians are united with Americans — they don't understand cricket. In fact, some Russians confuse it with croquet, because in their language the 't' is sounded in both words. Apart from this unfortunate deficiency, however, they are great people for sport and have produced many fine athletes. Funnily enough, the better they get at it, the more critical they become of their own players. If you are interested in and understand sport, this is one of the fields where you can have a critical discussion without feeling the other person is holding back for patriotic reasons.

what's on? There are a good many opportunities for watching sport and practising it. Apart from the 'keep fit' aspect, engaging in some of the Russians' outdoor pursuits makes you feel more at home in the country. But it's not so easy for the visitor to know what is on and where. All too often one learns that, say, Arsenal or Manchester United has been playing a Soviet team somewhere in Moscow only when the results come over on the nine o'clock news. If it's just rugby football that you're interested in, you may never find out, unless you comb the pages of *Sovetsky Sport* regularly. Some idea of what's on in Moscow can be gained from the English-language weekly *Moscow News*, and particularly *Moscow News Information*, which appears twice a week and announces some fixtures in advance. But here is a little basic information that may give you a clearer picture of what's on offer.

Both Association football (soccer) and Rugby **football**
Union football are now played in the USSR.
The latter is on a relatively modest scale, but
matches take place against teams from Eastern
Europe and the Soviet team has done well in
the European championship. American and
Canadian football are not played, nor is Rugby
League.

Both soccer and rugby are summer games
in the Soviet Union, though training starts
early in the southern republics. In Moscow
most important soccer matches take place at
the Lenin stadium, which lies in the great
bend of the Moscow River, opposite the Lenin
Hills. This stadium also has rugby pitches, but
international rugby matches are usually played
at the Fili ground, in Moscow's south-west.
Both stadiums are easily reached by Metro
(stations *Sportivnaya* and *Fili*).

When Russians talk about *hockyái*, they usually **hockey**
mean ice hockey, played with a puck according
to the international rules. But they have another
kind of their own, played with a ball on a
bigger rink, and usually outdoors. It's not so
fast as the international game, but its popularity
is growing, particularly in Scandinavia. In
Norway in 1985 a US team will compete in the
world championship.

Ice hockey is *the* game in winter. Over a

million play it at club level, and in yards and parks youngsters battle away for hours with almost none of the usual protective gear. The streets become deserted when the USSR is playing Canada or Czechoslovakia, its closest rivals for the world title, which has been in Soviet possession for years. If you want to see some of the best the game can offer, you have only to switch on your TV or visit the Lenin stadium during one of the annual inter-national tournaments.

skating and skiing

The great skating competitions have the added attraction that many more countries take part, including the United States and Britain, which often claims the honours in the dance. All such events, including the Winter Olympics, are, of course, televised.

Skiing, skating and toboganning are the obvious pastimes for a Russian winter. If you have never skied in your life, you need have no fears about starting in Moscow, because it is mostly over flat country and nearly all ages participate. Equipment can be hired cheaply in most of the big parks (Izmailovo and Sokolniki for skiing, Gorky Park for skating). For the downhill skier there are some short but tricky slopes in Fili park and on the Lenin Hills over-looking Moscow River, where incidentally there is also a giant international competition ski jump. Some hilly country at Skhodnaya can be reached by suburban train (from Leningrad-skaya Station). But for real mountain skiing you have to take time-off in the Caucasus, which is spectacular.

The sports shops offer a good deal of equipment at reasonable prices, but remember the old Russian saying about those who want to ride buying their sledge in summer. Actually early autumn is the best time for winter equipment.

All over the city there are workshops where *fitting*
you can have the bindings fitted to your skis. *yourself out*
A cross-country ski is the right length if you
can reach the tip when it is vertical. Sticks
should reach from floor level nearly up to
your armpits. Get a pair of boots that leave
room for one thick and one thin pair of
socks. But boots should not be loose, as they
stretch in the damp. Choose your bindings
according to the size of your boot, then take
all three elements to a workshop and have
them fitted together. It's quite tricky to do it
yourself, but they have a special bench to make
sure the boot is properly aligned along the ski.

There are facilities for riding, winter and summer, **riding**
at the Moscow Hippodrome (tel. 256 15 62).
The address is 22, Begovaya.

If you want instruction in the theory of
riding, you have to turn up at 8 a.m. in the
morning on Saturdays or Sundays — with an
interpreter unless you speak Russian. But
anyone familiar with the basic rules can take
out a horse for one rouble an hour from 8 a.m.
to 8 p.m. on any day of the week. A preliminary
visit is advisable to show the coach what you can
do and find out what horses are on offer.

Similar facilities, in more picturesque
surroundings, exist at the Urozhai centre in
Sokolniki Park (tel. 286 59 22) not far from
the International Exhibition, and the equestrian
sports centre in Bitsevo Park (Balaklavsky
Prospekt, 33, tel. 318 89 55).

Horse racing is not at all widespread. There
are trotting races at the hippodrome, where
you can have a bet on the state totalisator,
and that's about it. Racing has probably been
discouraged because of the betting aspect. On
the whole, there is very little gambling in the
USSR, except for the state premium bonds and
lotteries, tickets for which are on sale everywhere,

offering prizes of up to 10,000 roubles, motor cars, and so on. But the horse, after being practically eclipsed in economic importance by the tractor, looks like making a comeback in Soviet life.

show jumping

Show jumping is forging ahead. A course was opened in Bitsevo Park for the 1980 Olympics, and regular competitions are held there. At present the Lithuanians dominate this sport and riding is very popular in that republic. In the Caucasus it never died out, because of the terrain.

cycling

Russians either treat cycling as a serious sport or just cruise around in woods and parks for fun. There is very little cycle touring in the old sense, probably because of the heavy truck traffic and because the bicycle has been ousted by the motorbike and moped in the mind of youth. Now it is coming back, particularly the collapsible kind that can be put in the boot of a car. This is quite a good thing to bring from home if you fancy the idea of a spin in the woods, though you may have to carry your bike round several large puddles or fallen trees.

water sports
swimming

This is probably your best means of shaking off the effects of a life that because of cold outdoors and warmth indoors may become rather sedentary. Moscow has several heated pools, most of them run on a season ticket (*abonemènt*) basis (you will need a medical certificate — see below). The best kind are in the open air, with the water heated so effectively that swimming is quite pleasant even in the coldest weather (you reach the pool by plunging into a channel leading from the shower room). There may be ice and snow round the edges, but you don't feel it, and indeed you can hardly see it through the steam. A proper shower before and after is

obligatory, so you must take soap and something
to scrub yourself with. You will also need a
bathing cap (keeps your head warm) and a pair
of rubber sandals (to guard against foot
infection).

Some Russians, nicknamed walruses (*morzhêe*),
bathe in park lakes and rivers in mid winter.
There are special places where the ice is cleared
for this. But it's not a thing for Westerners to

indulge in without a doctor's advice and
probably a period of hardening. On the other
hand, the outdoor swimming in a heated pool
is recommended for all ages. Incidentally, you
have to get a medical certificate before they
will sell you a season ticket. No certificate is
required at the Moskva pool, where you can
buy a ticket on the day and also hire bathing
things.

sailing

In summer the numerous reservoirs round
Moscow are good places for swimming, the
favourites with both foreigners and Muscovites
being the Klyazma reservoir (up the Yaroslavl
road and turn left), and the Moscow River at
Serebryanny Bor (Khoroshevskoye Road). The
mile-wide Klyazma reservoir is nowadays dotted
with dinghies and wind-surfing boards. There
are parking facilities and camping is permitted
on the wooded shores. A ten-minute ride on the
Metro brings you to Izmailovo Park, in the

centre of which (quite a walk) are the lakes where Peter the Great sailed his first boats. They offer quite good bathing with a life-saving team in attendance, and scores of bathers, despite a rather curious notice beside one of the lakes saying 'no bathing permitted'. But don't venture in waters where nobody else is swimming, even if there is no prohibition. Russians undress uninhibitedly, but carefully, in the bushes, if there are no screens.

Zavidovo   The UPDK hunting lodge at Zavidovo, 117 km up the Leningrad Road, offers many sporting opportunities for diplomats, correspondents and business representatives and their guests. Situated at the confluence of the Shosha and Volga rivers, it offers excellent sailing, water skiing and swimming. For a reasonable charge your own boat will be looked after summer and winter, but you can also hire dinghies and rowing boats or cross the water by speedboat. On the other side of both rivers there are forests, which you can explore for mushrooms and berries.

Accommodation is in large or small chalets (rather expensive) or at the hotel (reasonable, a double room currently costs 18 r. a day). The grounds have various amusements for children, a tennis court, piers for fishing and swimming, and a site where you can camp for a small charge.

The shooting season for duck begins at dawn on the third Saturday of August, for grouse and geese on 1 September, for wild boar on 1 October, and for elk on 1 November, though whether licences are granted depends on the ecological situation at the time. All the equipment, and the services of a huntsman, can be hired.

The chalets have their own cooking facilities, but you can also eat in the hotel, which has a reasonably good restaurant, lounge and games rooms.

In winter you can skate in the grounds, ski long distances across the Volga and through the forests, or hire a mini-snocat and drive about. In fact, more people go for this kind of thing than for the shooting.

The place becomes fairly crowded at weekends, but is quiet during the week. If you have no car, you can travel up by train and arrange for a car to meet you at the station and take you the 7 or 8 km to the lodge.

For bookings at Zavidovo you have to contact UPDK (tel. 201 27 17). Weekday bookings may require only one day's notice, but allow longer for the weekends, and chalets have to be ordered a long time ahead. Permission to leave Moscow comes with the booking, but don't forget to mention your car registration number in your letter.

fishing

Fishing is a popular sport among Russians, even those who live in town. Since Moscow River was cleaned up, one can see hopeful anglers every day fishing from the embankment under the Kremlin walls. But for enjoyable sport you have to go further upstream. Where the good places are is something only the local people can tell you. Near Moscow you can't hope to catch anything bigger than roach or bream or perhaps an occasional pike. There are enthusiasts who like fishing through holes in the ice of lakes and rivers. This is an interesting experience if you have Russian friends who will introduce you to the pleasures of crouching on windswept ice and threading a worm on your hook before it or your fingers freeze — and who will assist you in defreezing yourself afterwards.

**cultural
scene**   Opera, ballet, concerts, the puppet theatres, and the circus are the main attractions for visitors who don't speak the language. In Moscow there are enough to keep you busy every night of the week. In the smaller cities the scope is much narrower but every republic has its national opera (which includes ballet) and conservatoire, while in some fields Leningrad and other cities of the Russian Federation rival Moscow. Some republics have strong national preferences, such as choral singing in Estonia.

Moscow has two permanent circus arenas, one in the centre of the city and the other on the Lenin Hills, where there is also a remarkable Children's Music Theatre.

ballet   In Moscow the main ballet companies are those of the Bolshoi Theatre (see p. 85 if you are intending to drive there), the Stanislavsky Opera and Ballet Theatre, and the Moscow Classical Ballet, which has no permanent stage yet and performs at the larger halls like Rossiya, when it is not on tour.

Leningrad has the Kirov Ballet (the former Imperial Ballet of St Petersburg) and the ballet of the Maly Opera Theatre. The cities of Novosibirsk, Baku, Perm, and Sverdlovsk also have notable ballet troupes. These companies bring their productions to Moscow and Leningrad from time to time, but for Soviet balletomanes a journey of a thousand miles to see the latest ballet sensation is nothing out of the ordinary. Admittedly, opinions differ widely about what is new or sensational and this is another field where you may expect some worthwhile critical discussion.

Every four years (1985 should be the next) there is an International Ballet Competition in Moscow, during which even the Bolshoi's strict rules of decorum go by the board and spectators stand on the plush divides between boxes when there is no room elsewhere. If you are a ballet enthusiast, you will soon find a kindred spirit who will put you in touch with the work of the smaller groups.

tickets

The only trouble is that Soviet people themselves are very keen on these entertainments. This means you may find it hard to get tickets, unless Intourist is looking after you or you have the privileges of an accredited newspaper correspondent or a senior diplomat. If you are in a less fortunate position, you must try to enlist the help of organisers at your place of study or work and at the same time pay regular visits to box-offices, theatre ticket kiosks, and theatre managers' offices. A letter on headed notepaper stating your needs (theatre research, for instance, see page 45), and presented to the manager in person, may yield more than just standing in a queue will achieve.

Soviet theatres and opera houses usually have a current repertoire of about ten productions which they repeat three or four times in the course of the month. Apart from any tickets that may be going at the box-office, they announce special ticket-selling days, when a batch of fresh tickets comes in. This is when you have to get up early and join the queue with an eye to obtaining something for the next two weeks or so. Some queues organise themselves so that early arrivals can get their name down on a list and come back later when the box office opens. Tickets are not expensive but there may be times when you wish they were.

music season tickets

It is not wise to take just any ticket that is offered at the theatre or the *estrada* (revue). But the season tickets offered at the conservatoires and other concert halls in early autumn are

bound to yield some good listening, although
the programmes they entitle you to are not
fully detailed. Season tickets can also be
bought for the Tchaikovsky Music Competition
(piano, violin, cello and singing) held in
Moscow every four years (next in 1986).
Intourist offers special tours for people from
abroad who want to attend such events.

performance
times
Evening performances at theatres nearly
always begin at 7 p.m. Concerts of classical
music start at 7.30. The Bolshoi Theatre (opera
and ballet) rings up the curtain very promptly
at 7 p.m. and you can expect to lose your seat
in the stalls for the first act if you are late,
even by only a few minutes, though you may
be able to stand in one of the upper boxes.
The conservatoires are equally strict.

Theatre matinées and matinée concerts start
at 12 noon.

'fringe'
and
experimental
performance
Compared with some Western capitals, there
are not many off-beat shows, but if you stay
long enough you may see some interesting
experimental work at theatre studios, and
on the second or third stages of the big theatres.
The revival of nineteenth-century classics as
musicals is now common practice, and the
version of the Tolstoy story *Strider* (Russian
Holstomer) by the Leningrad director
Tovstonogov is well known in the West. There
is a growing body of jazz and rock players
who perform at clubs, and this has resulted
in breakthroughs like the Lenin Komsomol
Theatre's rock opera *Yunon and Avos*, which
was filmed by the BBC.

fast music
If you like dancing to deafening music, this
can be had at many restaurants in the evening.
It may be worth trying to book by phone
beforehand and taking your passport to show
the doorman.

The cinema is still alive and well in the Soviet Union, although it has lost some ground to television. Quite a few foreign films are shown, including British and American. Unfortunately for the English speaker, they are usually dubbed into Russian. One cinema, currently the *Litva*, shows films in the original languages, but they may be rather old.

cinema

An International Film Festival is held in Moscow every two years.

Billboards all over the city give complete lists of which films are on, when and where. The films move around from district to district and disappear after two or three weeks, often to reappear in honour of some anniversary or at a *povtórny* (repeat) cinema.

Cinema performances are not continuous. For recent releases it is advisable to buy your ticket beforehand.

Moscow television has two channels, that start at 8 a.m. and bring you talks, music, drama, sport and news for the rest of the day. Of these, Channel 2 is mainly for the schools in the daytime. Education is also the main theme of Channel 4, which starts at 4 p.m. The Moscow Channel opens at 7 p.m. with a selection of talks, music and drama, accenting events in the capital. The main news on all channels is at 9 p.m. Colour TV employs a Soviet–French system, and Soviet and British sets are not compatible. There is no satisfactory Soviet video yet. Members of the foreign community import Western sets (JVC etc.) or buy them off each other and exchange videotapes among themselves. But with a JVC recorder (HD 120C) and a Sharp receiver it is possible to play back PAL cassettes and record Soviet programmes.

television

embassy club The British Embassy club shows films three times a week. It is at Kutuzovsky Prospekt 7/4 (opposite the Ukraina Hotel) and you may become an associate member if you hold a British passport and intend to stay in Moscow for at least a year. It also runs badminton, whist drives, Keep Fit classes, and so on. The Cultural Section of the embassy at the back of the main building (Nab. Morisa Toreza, 14) has a useful reading and information room and a lending library of English books that is open to British residents on Thursday afternoons (from 2 to 4 p.m.), when a thrift shop also functions.

There is also an International Women's Association open to all members of the foreign community in Moscow. It publishes a monthly *News* giving details of interest groups and other functions. It holds monthly meetings at one or another embassy. There is no subscription and one becomes a member simply by attending a meeting and putting one's name down. The US embassy club and cultural section are in the embassy itself, at Chaikovskovo 19/23.

museums and art galleries Museums and art galleries are numerous in Moscow, and even small towns usually have a local topographical museum or perhaps a 'house museum' (*dom moozyái*) connected with some famous personality who once lived there. Their opening times vary. Most of them begin at 10 or 11 a.m. and stay open till 5 or 6 p.m., but they may close much earlier in winter, particularly the former estates, such as the nineteenth-century mansion at Kuskovo, which closes at 3 p.m. from October to April. Museums and art galleries have cleaning days towards the end of the month and their rest day is usually Monday instead of Sunday. Make inquiries before undertaking a long trip.

What is a Soviet?

semantics

Most people will tell you it means 'council', but how it came to mean so many other things is something of a mystery. If you look up Webster's International, you will find the following definition: 'Soviets pl. usu. cap., the people, the leaders or the armed forces of the USSR.' I'm glad I didn't, accidentally, call this book 'Coping with the Soviets'.

In Russian the word 'soviet' has two meanings — 'council' and 'advice', and also the archaic sense of 'harmony' or 'wisdom'. People still wish their friends *'lyuboff da soviet'* (love and harmony) when they get married. So the word seems to have been the blood-brother of our own 'counsel' — except that we decided to differentiate the various meanings by using two spellings.

One sometimes wonders if our picture of the revolution might have been somewhat different if the word 'soviet' had been translated into English when the 'workers councils' emerged in 1917 as the new form of government. Instead, it was promptly absorbed without translation and we have had to live with the semantically encrusted English version ever since.

Incidentally, it *is* translated in the case of the 'Council of Ministers', to distinguish that body from the elected soviets, which now form the backbone of the country's administrative structure.

elections

The Soviet Union is a one-party state and there is no Opposition, but a lot of elections are held. The local Soviets are elected every two-and-a-half years. The Supreme Soviet of the USSR and the Supreme Soviets of the Union and Autonomous Republics are elected every five years. The Supreme Soviet of the USSR has two equal chambers, known as the Soviet of the Union and the Soviet of Nationalities, the first being elected on the basis of constituencies with equal populations, and the second consisting of 32 deputies from each Union Republic, 11 from each Autonomous Republic, 5 from each Autonomous Region, and one from each Autonomous Area. Altogether the present two chambers number 1499 deputies.

The Supreme Soviet of the USSR holds sessions twice a year and during the intervening periods its affairs are conducted by the Presidium which it elects.

Every Supreme Soviet also forms a Council of Ministers, which through its ministries (mining, transport, agriculture, etc.) is responsible for the administration and economic development of the republic or, in the case of the Council of Ministers of the USSR, the administration and economic development of the country as a whole.

Roughly speaking, the Supreme Soviet is the Parliament of the USSR, and the Council of Ministers may be regarded as the cabinet. The life of the Council coincides with that of the Supreme Soviet.

Compared with electioneering in the Western democracies, Soviet elections are rather quiet affairs. The point at issue is not whether there is to be a Conservative or Labour government for the next five years, but whether the candidates of the 'Communist and non-Party bloc' (a term indicating that though he or she may not necessarily be a Communist they support the party's policies) are fit to represent the interests of their constituents, whether they have a good record in public and private life, at their factory, laboratory, university, or whatever. The pre-election meeting at which a candidate for a local Soviet meets constituents is more like a company shareholders' meeting than the hustings. And in a sense this is what it is. Most of the voters have put their 'capital' (a working week of forty hours) into the district and they want to know what they will get out of it in terms of new shops, roads, housing, schools, etc.

You may live in Russia for a long time without having anything to do with these proceedings. But since they are of rather frequent occurrence (judges are similarly elected) it is worth knowing what all the flag-flying and music is about on an election day. Before polling takes place, canvassers come round urging people to cast their vote for the local candidate. If you happen to be living in a house with Soviet people, you may also be called on. Since the *agitátor* will probably be a schoolteacher or some other busy person performing a social service, it's only considerate to tell them you are not in on this event. The reason for the canvassers' activities is that, although legally the candidate requires only a straight majority to be elected, anything less than 95 per cent of the votes would be considered a very poor showing. It is rare for a candidate not to be elected, but they occasionally disgrace themselves and are recalled from office by their constituents.

There are between 18 and 19 million people in the Communist Party of the USSR, which is described in the Constitution as the 'leading and guiding force of Soviet society'. This means that one in every thirteen or fourteen adults you meet is likely to be a Party member. In the diplomatic corps and foreign trade organisations the percentage may be a good deal higher. It's not all that easy to get into the party. A lot

the Communist Party

of questions are asked about one's private and public life, there is a lengthy period of probation, one's work record is crucial, and from the moment of being accepted one is expected to carry out all kinds of assignments, from working late hours to moving home and family to the other side of the country to fill a gap in the apparatus.

The structure of the party apparatus parallels that of the Soviets, but its function is ideological rather than administrative. In other words, through its members at all levels, it initiates movements that ultimately result in the passing of laws by the Soviets. Hence the importance of the Party Congress (irregular in Stalin's time but now held every five years). The Congress may amend the party programme, and though couched in general terms, such amendments often signal numerous extremely concrete changes in the administration and economy.

The Communist Party is controlled by its Central Committee, a body of about 200 senior party members elected by the Party Congress. The Central Committee forms a Politburo of up to 15 members, which makes all crucial policy decisions. The Politburo is headed by the General Secretary of the Communist Party. Relations between the Politburo, the Presidium of the Supreme Soviet and the Council of Ministers are far too complicated a subject for this book. Suffice it to say that the need for the Soviet Union to have an effective Head of State has led to the offices of chairman of the Supreme Soviet Presidium and General Secretary of the Communist Party often being vested in one person.

trade unions A few words about the trade unions are needed to complete this brief summary of the public organisations that play an important part in Russian lives and may, if you happen to be involved businesswise with a Soviet organisation, have a bearing on your relations with it.

There are trade union committees at every Soviet factory, coal mine, ministry, university, or whatever. There is one at UPDK. The functionaries of these committees are elected every year by union members. Membership is open to anyone on the staff of the organisation concerned. Everybody who joins has to pay monthly dues amounting to one per cent of that month's earnings to trade union funds and be prepared to take some part in the union's activities.

Based on the local union committee (*mestkom*), the trade union structure is topped by the All-Union Central Council of Trade Unions. The unions have a budget of their own and also administer state social insurance spending on pensions, building of health resorts, and so on.

At local level the trade union committee is mainly concerned with working conditions, the intricacies of innovation in production, health care, provision for staff holidays and leisure activities. It has a right to veto management decisions on dismissals. Disputes are settled by the factory's or the department's arbitration commission, a body on which management and union are equally represented. If no agreement follows, the employee can take the management to court.

Settling In

People staying in the USSR for any length of time usually live in flats. If yours is in a block specially reserved for foreigners, you will probably be well looked after. But a few hints on how to look after yourself may still apply, whether your accommodation is in a foreigner's house or one where most of the other tenants are Soviet.

DEZ The first thing you have to do is to establish yourself in residence by going to the local DEZ (housing maintenance office formerly ZHEK), showing them your passport and residence permit and collecting the books you will need for paying your rent, electricity, telephone, etc. The DEZ is usually in one of the flats on the ground floor of your block, or a block near by, and will be open at various times on various days of the week. For the larger apartment blocks there will be someone on duty all day, and it's a good thing to get their phone number, so that you can contact them when something goes wrong in the flat or the lift is out of order.

The DEZ is responsible for your electricity, water (including hot water) supply, and heating. It also looks after the exterior of the building, the doors, staircases and lifts, and rubbish disposal. The cost of these services is included in your rent, but you should tip people who do minor repairs in your flat, especially the plumber. Plumbers are notorious for not turning up when needed, if they feel they haven't been treated properly.

Gas is supplied and maintained by the municipal gas authority, in Moscow known as

MOSGAZ. Their emergency number is 04, but if the trouble is not urgent 04 will give you a local number.

paying bills

A Russian rent book is a rather simple affair, consisting of bills and counterfoils that you fill in yourself. The people at the DEZ will fill in your first page for you with the sums due. You take it to the local branch of the state bank (*sherkássa*). pay your money, the clerk puts the book in a machine which stamps both bill and counterfoil, keeps the bill and gives you back the book with the counterfoil stamped. The next month you copy the information given on the counterfoil on to the next page and repeat the process. Gas is not metered but electricity is, so you have to read the electricity meter. It should be just inside your front door, but in modern houses it is often just outside. You take the kWh reading, subtract the previous reading and multiply the difference by four. This gives you the amount due for electricity in kopecks. Gas is paid at a flat rate of 42 kopecks per person per month, so you multiply according to the number of persons in the flat and add the result to your electricity bill.

Bills for long-distance telephone calls come in the mail and you pay them in the same way. Be prompt about paying telephone bills and pay in advance if you are going away. Otherwise your phone may be cut off and it will be quite a job to get it back. In other respects the authorities are surprisingly lenient about arrears. Some Russians default for months or even years, but it's not the thing for a visitor to do.

The charges for diplomatic flats are much higher than ordinary Soviet rates (to bring them into line with equivalent services abroad). UPDK sends the bills, which are paid either direct (Kursovoy 1) or through the state bank.

window
sealing
The advantages of double glazing are now appreciated even in England. But double and even treble window frames have a long history in Russia and there are several different types. When the wind is blowing straight at it, even a well heated room with double glazing can become quite chilly unless you seal the cracks round the window frames. An old-fashioned window with a small hinged ventilation pane (*fortochka*) is easily sealed with strips of white paper that you can buy at any stationer's. The traditional adhesive is potato flour mixed to a paste with water, because it comes off easily in spring. But the more modern type of full-length window that has to be opened for ventilation often needs additional strips of foam round the edges. A reel of narrow window sealing with an adhesive backing is a good thing to bring from home. If even after that the room is still cold at times, buy an electric bowl fire or an electric oil-filled radiator.

ventilation
On the other hand, in many flats there is no way of adjusting the heat from radiators, which may be supplied from a central heating plant (*teplotsentral*) some distance away and regulated by a central thermostat. So you may find yourself jumping out of bed in the middle of the night to open a window, then getting up again half an hour later to shut out an icy draught. A way out of this difficulty is to buy a window spring with an arm that keeps the window shut without your fastening the catch. You then attach a cord to the window, so that you can pull it open from your bed, when you need air. Loop the cord over a bedpost, chair or some other solid object and release it to let the window spring shut when you've had enough. With practice this can be achieved almost without waking up.

All sealing operations and having your

windows cleaned need to be done before the cold weather sets in, which can be early in October.

walls

You will probably want to put a few nails or screws into your walls, for hanging pictures, fixing shelves, etc. The ferro-concrete panel used for the exterior and supporting walls of many modern blocks can only be pierced by a powerful drill with a hardened (*pobeditovy*) tip. Unless you have one of these, it's better to ask the local DEZ to send up someone who can do the job. It will cost you only a few roubles. The same applies to the prefabricated hard-wall plaster of modern bathrooms and toilets. But other walls in new houses are usually made of a softish material known as gypsolite and take nails quite well. To make a strong fixture, however, you need some sort of plug (*próbka*), usually available, complete with screws, in hardware stores. If you have plasterboard walls, tap the spot you have chosen to make sure you don't knock the nail into a hollow section.

fuses and voltage

Most of the Soviet Union works on 220V, but there are still a few pockets of 127V even in Moscow. Modern blocks often have trip-fuses that you can restore by flicking a switch, located next to your electricity meter. But older houses have ceramic fuses that screw into sockets in the fuse box. You can buy these in electrical shops and keep them in readiness for the time when you blow a fuse with a faulty iron or table lamp. Then, if you don't know which is which, you just go on changing the fuses until the lights come on again. If a fuse hasn't been changed for so long that it won't unscrew, call the DEZ electrician. Of course, handy people can simply replace the fuse wire on the ceramic core. Friendly neighbours, particularly the younger members of the family, are good at this. But they sometimes put in a thick wire that results in a black-out for the whole staircase the next time you have a short circuit.

burglar alarms The risk of your flat being burgled is not very great. Diplomatic flats have security men on duty at gateways who check up on the identity of any stranger. But if you live in an ordinary Soviet flat and are nervous about break-ins, you can have a simple kind of burglar alarm installed for a small charge. It consists of a siren which is triggered a minute after the front door opens and doesn't stop until you operate an easily visible but rather tricky switch. The theory runs that the thief is usually scared off by the noise of the siren and, even if he knows how to stop it, has no means of telling whether the device is not also sending a signal to the militia (i.e., police). At all events the militia claim that very few thefts have been carried out in flats equipped with this system.

insurance You can also insure yourself against theft, fire or other damage to your property with the state insurance company Ingosstrakh. The premium for a policy covering you against theft, fire and flood is at present 0.01% of the value of the goods as stated by the owner. If you pay it in hard currency you are compensated in the same.

health The Soviet medical system differs from ours in having no general practitioners. You go to a 'polyclinic', where, if you have several things wrong with you, or they think you may have, you are passed from specialist to specialist — ear nose and throat (*laringólog*), broken bones (*hirórg*), skin (*dermatólog*), and so on. The doctor you see for general advice is the *terapévt*, who has nothing to do with occupational or psychiatric therapy, but is a specialist in internal diseases and, if necessary, can coordinate the findings of the others. If it's psychiatric advice that you need, you go to a *nevropatólog* (neurologist), but Soviet doctors are reluctant to undertake treatment in cases of long-term psychiatric troubles.

All this is not the ultimate in specialisation. If you have some baffling health problem, you may be given an appointment with a higher expert in the field, known as a *professor*.

As soon as you start going to a polyclinic, they start up a book on you, in which all the specialists write their reports. This book is kept in their files and whenever you give your name at the reception desk a nurse finds it and takes it to whichever doctor you need. It's a good system and works well, but for anyone with hypochondriac tendencies it can be a snare and a temptation. You can spend days on end going from one doctor to another.

Russians are great believers in physiotherapy, and what they call 'resort' cures, i.e., going to the Caucasus for mud or mineral baths, breathing the air of the Crimea for lung troubles, and so on. Courses of treatment for people from abroad can be organised through Intourist.

home remedies

Russian doctors often recommend vitamin tablets, and their drugs industry produces large quantities in various combinations. But some Russians love to ply you with remedies of their own, among which vodka often gets pride of place.

Vodka is said to be an excellent antiseptic — quite true. It can be used to make a compress to relieve inflammation — also true. It cures a cold? Perhaps, but not if you have a sore throat (makes it worse), or if you have to go out in the cold after drinking it. The deceptive thing about vodka is that you may feel good, but your body is losing heat up to three times faster than when you are sober. Which is why people who get drunk and fall asleep in the snow sometimes don't wake up. Safer methods of 'sweating it out' are hot drinks made of lemon, dried raspberries, and so on, but they all require a good night's sleep in a warm bed.

Russian grandmothers, and some doctors, are always keen on your applying mustard plasters (*gorcheechniks*) to clear up a cold or stop it getting on to your chest. And, surprisingly, granny's method often works. You buy *gorcheechniks* for a few kopecks at the chemists.

sea buckthorn Among the numerous herbal remedies a much-sought-after panacea is oil from the berry of sea buckthorn, said to be good for healing tissues. It grows in mountainous regions and is now being widely cultivated. There must be something in sea buckthorn berries because the state has recently started manufacturing a toothpaste (Zodiac) with their oil as an ingredient. Incidentally, it also grows on the south coast of the UK.

tourist and diplomatic clinics If a tourist needs to see a doctor, Intourist will arrange things in any city. Treatment is free but some medicines may have to be paid for. In Moscow the tourists' polyclinic (tel. 254 43 96) is about five minutes' walk from the Byelorussia Station Metro. It also caters for a lot of people from abroad who are permanently resident in the USSR — students, employees of Soviet organisations, and so on.

There is a large new polyclinic for diplomats and other people accredited with the Ministry for Foreign Affairs near the Dobryninskaya Metro (tel. 237 59 33). At this clinic you pay for consultation and treatment unless your

country has an umbrella health agreement
with the USSR, which Britain has.

Both polyclinics will send a doctor if you
are not well enough to go to them. There is
also an emergency ambulance service for the
whole city, which can be called on 03.

If you arrive in the USSR from Britain or the **inoculations**
USA, you don't need any International Certificates of vaccination. But visitors from Asia,
South America or Africa must have one against
smallpox and, in some cases, against cholera
as well.

The Soviet health service is highly organised
and the authorities sometimes launch campaigns
for getting everybody inoculated against
Asiatic flu (*grippe*) or other epidemics that may
hit the USSR. You usually get word of this
through your place of work. But since the
effectiveness of vaccination against flu has
yet to be conclusively proved, no one will
insist if you don't want to have it. In the rare
event of a cholera scare, however, it's better
to take what's offered.

You are allowed to bring pets into the USSR   **pets**
provided they have a clean bill of health from
the country of origin. In the case of dogs a
certificate of inoculation against hepatitis,
plague and rabies is also advisable, unless you
are prepared to have your dog given the
standard composite jab on arrival. For more
exotic pets make full inquiries beforehand.

Only a few years ago a majority of urban
Russians were opposed to dogs in cities, but
their popularity has rocketed recently (partly
due to a famous book and film *Beem*, about
an English setter). Some Russians, however,
particularly mothers, regard all dogs as a
menace and it would be unwise to bring any
but a friendly, adaptable animal into the

country. You will have to get your pet registered at the local veterinary polyclinic and obey various by-laws about where you can walk it.

going to church

Anglicans and Protestants have opportunities for worship at services held in the British Embassy and at Spasso House (residence of the American ambassador) on alternate Sundays at 10 a.m. in summer and 10.30 a.m. in winter.

Baptists hold services on Sundays at 10 a.m., 2 p.m. and 6 p.m. at Maly Vuzovsky 3 (tel. 297 51 67).

Mass is celebrated in Latin with sermons in Polish and Russian at Malaya Lubyanka 12, and in English and French at Kutuzovsky 7/4, apt. 42 (tel. 243 96 21).

There is a mosque at Vipolzov 7 (near Metro Prospekt Mira), at which prayers are recited five times daily and on Fridays at 1 p.m. For information about the Muslim religion in other parts of the country one should contact the Foreign Relations Department of Muslim Organisations in the USSR, Metrostroyevskaya 49, Moscow (tel. 248 68 69).

The Greek Orthodox Church of the Archangel Gabriel is at Telegrafny 15a. There is a Synagogue at Arkhipovka 8.

In Moscow between thirty and forty Russian Orthodox churches hold regular services on Sundays and during the week. There is some particularly fine choir singing to be heard at the Yelokhovsky Cathedral, Spartakovskaya 5, and at the Church of All the Sorrowful (*Vsekh Skorbyàschikh*), Bolshaya Ordynka 20, where the little-known liturgies composed by Tchaikovsky and Rachmaninoff are sometimes performed.

Russian Orthodox Christmas (*rozhdestvò*) is celebrated according to the old calendar (13 days behind ours) and falls on 7 January.

Easter (*páskha*) may sometimes coincide with
that of the Western Church but more often
comes one, four or five weeks later. Russian
Orthodox Christians observe the fast (*post*)
during Lent and before Christmas, and some
of the ancient customs connected with the
Saviour's days 1, 6 and 16 August, according
to the old calendar. These Saviour's-day
festivals are linked with farming traditions
and the soil. The first is known as *medóvy
spas* (honey feast), when the hives are opened,
the second as *yáblochny* (apple), when the apples
are picked and eaten for the first time, and the
third as *polotnyány* (linen, the miracle of
Christ's image appearing on cloth), after which
the winter wheat is sówn. Full details of
Orthodox worship can be obtained from the
Moscow Patriarchate at Chistiy per. 5 (tel.
201 23 40).

Most people who come to Russia with their **education**
families send their children to the Anglo-
American School, the Ecole Française or one
of the other foreign schools. The fees are high
but compensation is usually paid by the
parents' employer – embassy, business firm, and
so on.

It is quite possible, however, to have your
child educated at a Soviet school free of charge.
Soviet children start school at the age of seven
and the full course takes them up to the age of
eighteen. Recent reforms propose reducing the
entrance age to six.

Discipline is reasonably good and no physical
punishment is allowed. Some schools have an
English 'bias', which means that some subjects,
besides English, are taught in English. For
children who show exceptional ability there are
specialised schools (*spétsshkóla*) that teach
music or mathematics along with other subjects
up to a high academic standard.

the day
nothing
works

During a long Russian winter there are bound to be some days when you feel lackadaisical and depressed. The sky is leaden but it won't snow. The ground is hard and lumpy and a bitter wind whips the dust off it into your face. The letter you have been expecting for weeks is still not in the letterbox. You enter your flat with the intention of having a long, luxurious shower, but for some reason the hot water has been turned off. At such times most Russians would say 'Try a Russian bath'.

There are still quite a few public baths all over Moscow, and the Sandunovsky Baths retain much of their old-world splendour. In smaller cities they play an even more important part in everyday life. In some republics, particularly the Baltic, the Scandinavian sauna is becoming popular. But the traditional Russian bath relies on hot-water pipes and steam.

Besides soap and towels, you should take something to rub yourself down with. Russians often take a bunch of birch twigs with the leaves still on them to whack themselves. In the heat the leaves give off rather a comforting smell.

The first room is usually pretty warm and has numerous hot and cold taps, hand-tubs and benches where you can wash yourself at leisure. The second room is hot enough to make anyone sweat, and there is an even hotter room with a shelf where the temperature is so high that you can't stay there more than a few minutes, after which you return to more moderate heat, douching yourself as you go. It's a good thing to be with friends, so that you can help each other with the rubbing down or whacking. And it's nice to have someone to talk to in a place where most people seem to know each other. But at good baths you can usually hire a washer who will get you on a stone slab, cover you in soap and pummel you into shape. After that you take a rest and time to cool down before getting dressed.

The effect is certainly relaxing. When you come out, the wind will seem less vicious, there may be soft snowflakes in the air, and at home you are almost sure to find that the hot water has come on again.

Some Simple Words and Questions

(Remember the Russian 'o', when not stressed, sounds like 'u' in 'but')

words	accident	авария	avariya
	actor	актёр	aktyór
	actress	актриса	aktréessa
	address	áдрес	ádres
	after	после	póslye
	agency	агéнтство	agéntsvo
	airmail	áвиа	áviya
	airport	аэропóрт	aeropórt
	all	всё	vsyo
	America	Амéрика	Amérika
	American	американский	amerikánsky
	American (man)	американец	amerikánets
	American (woman)	американка	amerikánka
	and	и	ee
	antibiotics	антибиóтики	antibiótiky
	Australian	австралийский	avstraléesky
	baby	бэ́би, ребёнок	báibee, rebyónok
	back	назáд	nazád
	bad	плóхо	plókho
	baker's	бýлочная	bóolochnaya
	ballet	балéт	balyét
	bank	банк	bank
	bed	кровáть	krováat
	beer	пиво	péevo
	before	пéред	péryed
	block (of flats)	кóрпус	kórpus
	big	большóй	bulshóy
	bill	счёт	shchot
	book	книга	knéega

bread	хлеб	hleb
breakfast	за́втрак	závtrak
bridge	мост	most
Britain	Вели́кобрита́ния	Velíkobritániya
Britisher	брита́нец	britányets
buffet	буфе́т	boofyét
bus	автобус	avtóbus
butter	ма́сло	máslo

cabbage	капу́ста	kapóosta
café	кафе́	cafái
camping	ке́мпинг	kémping
campsite	ке́мпинг	kémping
Canadian	кана́дский	kanádsky
car	автомоби́ль,	avtomobéel,
	маши́на	mashéena
case	чемода́н	chemodán
caviare	икра́	eekráh
chauffeur	шофёр	shufyór
chemist's	апте́ка	aptéka
choir	хор	hor
church	це́рковь	tsérkoff
cigarette	сигаре́та	tsigarétta
cinema	кино́	keenó
circus	цирк	tsirk
clean	чи́сто	chéesto
code	код	kawd
(front-door)		
code	код	kawd
(telephone)		
code	и́ндекс	éendeks
(postal)		
coffee	ко́фе	cáwfye
colour	цвет	tsvet
concert	конце́рт	kuntsért
crossroads	перекрёсток	perekryóstok
cucumber	огуре́ц	ugooréts

dancing	та́нцы	tántsi
dinner	обе́д	ubyéd
doctor	до́ктор	dáwkta
dollar	до́ллар	dáwla
draught	сквозня́к	skvuznyák
drink	пить	peet

early	ра́но	ráano
eat	есть	yaist
English (British)	англи́йский	angléesky
Englishman	англича́нин	anglichánin
Englishwoman	англича́нка	anglichánka
enough	доста́точно	dustátochno
evening	ве́чер	vyécher
film (camera)	плёнка	plyónka
film (cinema)	кинофи́льм	keenoféelm
floor (storey)	эта́ж	etáge
football	футбо́л	footbáll
fork	ви́лка	veelka
friend	друг	droog
friendship	дру́жба	dróozhba
fruit	фру́кты	fróokti
garage (storage)	гара́ж	garázh
garage (repair)	техста́нция	tekhstántsiya
glad	рад	raat
glass	стака́н	stakáan
good	хоро́ший	huróshy
greetings	приве́т	preevyét
guest	гость	gost
haircut	стри́жка	stréeshka
hairdresser	парикма́херская	pareekmákherskaya
hard (firm)	жёсткий	zhóstky
headache	головна́я боль	guluvnáya boil
help	по́мощь	pómoshch
hockey	хокке́й	hockyái
holiday		
(public)	пра́здник	prázdnik
(leave)	отпуск	otpoosk
hospital	больни́ца	bulnéetsa
hotel	гости́ница	gustéenitsa
hour	час	chas
house	дом	dom
hunting	охо́та	aháwta
ice	лёд	lyod
icecream	моро́женое	murózhennoye
ignition	зажига́ние	zazhigániye

influenza	грипп	greep
information	информация	informátsiya
Ireland	Ирландия	Irlándiya
Irish	ирландский	irlándsky
journalist	журналист	zhoornaléest
juice	сок	sok
knife	нож	nozh
kopeck	копейка	kupyáika
Kremlin	кремль	kreml
lane (sidestreet)	переулок	pereóolok
late	поздно	pózdno
leak	утечка	ootéchka
left	лево	lyévo
lemonade	лимонад	leemonád
letter	письмо	peesmó
lettuce	салат	saláat
lift	лифт	leeft
love	любовь	lyubóff
lovely	чудесный	choodésny
luck (also happiness)	счастье	schástye
luggage	багаж	bagázh
lunch	обед	ubyéd
manager	администратор	administrátor
map	карта	kárta
market	рынок	rínok
medicine	лекарство	lekárstvo
meeting	встреча	vstrécha
menu	меню	menyú
Metro	метро	metró
milk	молоко	mulukó
money	деньги	déngy
museum	музей	moozyái
name	имя	éemya
new	новый	náwvee
newspaper	газета	gazéta
New Zealand	новозеландский	nóvozelándsky
no	нет	nyet
not	не	nye
number (of room, house)	номер	náwmyer

old	ста́рый	stáry
open	откры́то	utkríto
other, another	друго́й	droogóy
parcel	посы́лка	pusílka
park (amenity)	парк	park
park (for cars)	стоя́нка	stoyánka
person	челове́к	chelovék
plan	план	plaan
plane	самоле́т	samulyót
please	пожа́луйста	pozhálsta
potato	карто́фель	kartófel
post office	по́чта	póchta
pound	фунт	foont
present	пода́рок	pudárok
question	вопро́с	vuprós
quick	бы́стро	bístro
radio	ра́дио	rádeeo
rain	дождь	dozhd
ready	гото́во	gutáwvo
record	пласти́нка	plastéenka
Red Square	Кра́сная Пло́щадь	Krásnaya plóshchad
restaurant	pecтоpа́н	restorán
right	пра́во	právo
road	доро́га, щоссе́	duráwga, chaussée
rouble	ру́бль	róoble
rugby	ре́гби	régby
Russian	ру́сский	róosky
salmon	сёмга	syómga
salt	соль	soil
school	шко́ла	shkóla
Scottish	шотла́ндский	shotlándsky
self-service	са́мообслу́живание	samoobslóozhivaniye
shop	магази́н	magazéen
shower	душ	doosh
shut	закры́то	zakríto
skating	ката́ние на конька́х	katániye na kunkakh
sleep	спать	spaat
snow	снег	snekh

soap	мы́ло	mílo
soft	мя́гкий	myágkhy
sorry	винова́т	veenovát
spoon	ло́жка	lóshka
sport	спорт	sport
square	пло́щадь	plóshchad
station	вокза́л	vugzál
stop	стоп, остано́вка	stop, ustanóvka
street	у́лица	óolitsa
sugar	са́хар	sákhar
sun	со́лнце	sólntsa
swimming pool	бассе́йн	bassyáin

table	стол	stol
taxi	такси́	taksée
tea	чай	chigh (like 'high')
teacher	учи́тель	oochéetel
telegram	телегра́мма	telegrámma
telephone	телефо́н	telefón
television	телеви́дение	televéedeniye
thank you	спаси́бо	spaséebo
that	тот	tot
theatre	теа́тр	tyeátr
this	э́то	éto
time	вре́мя	vrémya
today	сего́дня	sevódnya
toilet	туале́т	tualyét
tomorrow	за́втра	závtra
towel	полоте́нце	puluténtsye
town	го́род	górod
train	по́езд	póyezd
tram	трамва́й	tramvígh
trolleybus	тролле́йбус	trollyáibus

Ukrainian	укра́инский	ookráinsky
umbrella	зопт	zont
underground	метро́	Metró
up	вверх	vverkh
urgent	сро́чно	sróchno
USA (United States)	США (Соединённые Штаты)	Shah

vegetables	о́вощи	óvoshchy
vegetarian	вегетариа́нец	vegeteriánets

| view | вид | veet |
| vodka | во́дка | vódka |

wait	ждать	zhdat
waiter	официа́нт	offitsiánt
waitress	официа́нтка	offitsiántka
water	вода́	vudá
weather	пого́да	pugóda

| Welsh | уэ́льсский | wélsky |
| wine | вино́ | veenó |

year	год	gawt
yes	да	da
yesterday	вчера́	vcherá
young	молодой	muludóy

zero	ноль	noil
zip	мо́лния	mólniya
zoo	зоопа́рк	zopárk

Questions   If you are lucky, you may receive a brief reply.

How?	Как?	kak?
How are you?	Как вы?	kak vi?
How is he?	Как он?	kak on?
How is the weather?	Как пого́да?	kak pugóda?

| How much, many? | Ско́лько? | skólko? |
| How much does it cost? | Ско́лько сто́ит? | skólko stóeet? |

| What? | Что? | shto? |
| What is it? | Что э́то? | shto éto? |

Which?	Како́й?	kakóy?
Which bus?	Како́й авто́бус?	kakóy avtóbus?
Which floor?	Како́й эта́ж?	kakóy etáge?
What address?	Како́й а́дрес?	kakóy ádres?

When?	Когда́?	kugdá?
When does it start?	Когда́ нача́ло?	kugdá nachálo?
When does it end?	Когда́ коне́ц?	kugdá kunéts?
When is the train?	Когда́ по́езд?	kugdá póyezd?

Where?	Где?	gdye?
Where is the restaurant?	Где ресторáн?	gdye restorán?
Where is the Metro?	Где метрó?	gdye metró?

Where to?	Кудá?	koodá?
Where are we going?	Кудá ты?	koodá mi?
Where does this bus bus go?	Кудá э́тот автóбус?	koodá étot? avtóbus?

Who?	Кто?	kto?
Who are you?	Кто вы?	kto vi?
Who is he?	Кто он?	kto on?

Conversions and Sizes

conversions
temperature

To convert Fahrenheit into Centigrade, subtract 32, then multiply by $5/9$.

Centigrade into Fahrenheit, multiply by $9/5$, then add 32.

Centigrade	Fahrenheit
40	104
36.5	98.4 (blood heat)
30	86
20	68
10	50
0	32
−10	14
−20	−4
−30	−22

weight
100 grammes = 3.33 ozs; 1 kilo = 2.2 lbs
1 oz = 28.35 g.; 4 lb = 0.45 kg

length
1 centimetre = 0.39 inches; 1 metre = 39.37 inches
1 inch = roughly 2.5 cm

distance
1 kilometre = 0.62 (about $5/8$) miles
1 mile = 1.61 km
10 km = roughly 6 miles

liquid
1 litre = 1.76 imperial pints or 2.11 US pints
1 imp. pint = 0.57 litres; 1 imp. gallon = 4.55 litres
1 US pint = 0.47 litres; 1 US gallon = 3.79 litres

petrol consumption
30 mpg (imp.) = 24 mpg (US) = 9.1 litres to 100 km (approx. consumption of Soviet Lada saloon)

dresses and suits

British	10	12	14	16	18	20	22
US	8	10	12	14	16	18	20
Soviet	40	42	44	46	48	50	52

shoes

British	2½	3	4	5	6	7	8
US	4	4½	5½	6½	7½	8½	9½
Soviet	35	36	37	38	39	40	41

clothing sizes *women*

suits and overcoats

British and US	36	38	40	42	44	46
Soviet	46	48	50	52	54	56

men

shirts

British and US	14	14½	15	15½	16	16½	17
Soviet	36	37	38	39	41	42	43

shoes

British	7	7½	8	8½	9	9½	10
US	8½	9	9½	10	11½	12	12½
Soviet	39	40	41		42	43	44

hats

British and US	6½	6⅝	6¾	6⅞	7	7⅛	7¾	7³/₈	7½
Soviet	53	54	55	56	57	58	59	60	61

Useful Addresses

Australia   *CBC Travel Service*
10 Petrie Street
Canberra City
ACT 2601

Intourist UK Ltd
Underwood House
37–49 Pitt Street
Sydney 2000
(tel. 277652)

Orbit Travel Services Pty Ltd
116 King Street
Sydney, NSW 2000

Orbit House
183–5 Elizabeth Street
Melbourne 3000

Palanga Travel Ltd
280 Pitt Street
Sydney 2000

Britain   *Aeroflot Soviet Airlines*
69/72 Picadilly
London W1
(tel. 01 493 7436)

Anglo-Soviet Shipping Co. Ltd
Scottish Union House
10 Lloyds Avenue
London EC3
(tel. 01 488 2466)

Barry Martin Travel
324 Regent Street
London W1R 5AA
(tel. 01 637 0373)

Black Sea and Baltic General Insurance Co. Ltd
65 Fenchurch Street
London EC3M 4EY
(tel. 01 709 9202)

British—Soviet Chamber of Commerce
2 Lowndes Street
London SW1X 9ET
(tel. 01 235 2423/4)

British—Soviet Friendship Society
36 St John's Square
London EC1 4JH
(tel. 01 253 4161)

Collets Bookshop
129/131 Charing Cross Road
London WC2H 0EQ
(tel. 01 734 0782/3)

East European Trade Council
25 Victoria Street
London SW1H 0EX
(tel. 01 222 7622)

Great Britain—USSR Association
14 Grosvenor Place
London SW1
(tel. 01 235 2116)

Intourist Moscow Ltd
292 Regent Street
London W1R 7PO
(tel. 01 631 1252 (administration)
     01 580 1221 (reservations))

Intourist Moscow Ltd (Manchester)
71 Deansgate
Manchester M3 2EY
(tel. 061 8340230)

Moscow Narodny Bank
24—32 King William Street
London EC4P 4JS
(tel. 01 623 2066)

Overseas Trade Division
Department of Trade
1 Victoria Street
London SW1H 0ET
(tel. 01 215 5265, telex 27366)

Society for Cultural Relations with the USSR
320 Brixton Road
London SW9 6AB
(tel. 01 274 2282)

Soviet Consulate
5 Kensington Palace Gardens
London W8
(tel. 01 229 3215/6)

Soviet Embassy
18 Kensington Palace Gardens
London W8
(tel. 01 229 6412)

Canada   *Intourist*
1801 McGill College Av.
Suite 630
Montreal
Quebec H3A 2N4
(tel. (514) 849 6394, telex 055—62018)

Globe Tours
1066 Bloor Street West
Toronto
Ontario M6H 1M6

Globe Tours
615 Selkirk Avenue
Winnipeg
Manitoba R2W 2N2

Globe Tours
2679 East Hastings Street
Vancouver 6, BC

Finnair
8 King Street East
Toronto
Ontario M5C 1B5

Romantic Tours Ltd   **Hong Kong**
807 Melbourne Plaza
Queen's Road C.
Hong Kong

Wallem Shipping (Hong Kong) Ltd
48th Floor Hopewall Center
183 Queen's Road E.
PO Box 40
Hong Kong

Trade Representation of the USSR in India   **India**
Representation of *Intourist*, Plot 6 and 7
block 50E
Nyaya Marg Chanakyapuri, New Delhi 110021
(tel. 699105/6/7)

Mercury Travels (India) PVT Ltd
Jeevan Tara Building
Gate 4–A, Ground Floor
Parliament Street
New Delhi 110001

International Travel Consortium
39 Nariman Bhavan
227 Nariman Point
Bombay 400 021

Trade Wings (Private) Ltd
60 Janpath Road
New Delhi 110001

Atlantic and Pacific Travel International Ltd   **New**
Parnell Place   **Zealand**
164 Parnell Road
Auckland

Atlantic and Pacific Travel Ltd
PO Box 3030
Wellington

Atlantic and Pacific
131 Cashel Street
Christchurch

Globetrotter Tours (NZ) Ltd
1 St Luke Square
Mt Albert
PO Box 41—004
Auckland

United   *Aeroflot*
States 545 5th Avenue
New York, NY 10017
(tel. 212 661 4050)

American Council of Teachers of Russian
Russian Center
815 New Guelph Road
Bryn Mawr,
Philadelphia, PA 19010

Amtorg Trading Corporation
750 3rd Avenue
New York, NY 10017
(tel. 212 972 1220)

Barry Martin Travel Inc.
19 West Street, 34th Floor
New York, NY 10004
(tel. 212 422 0091)

Citizens Exchange Council
10th Floor
18 East 41st Street
New York, NY 10017

Consular Office USSR Embassy
1825 Phelps Place NW
Washington DC 20008
(tel. 202 332 1483)
(see also *Soviet Consulate General*)

Council of International Education and Exchange
205 East 42nd Street
New York, NY 10010

*Council for International Exchange of Scholars
(Fulbright Program)*
11 Dupont Circle NW
Washington DC 20036

Intourist
Rockefeller Center
630 Fifth Avenue, Suite 868
New York, NY 10111

IREX (International Research Exchange)
655 Third Avenue
New York, NY 10017

*National Council for American–Soviet Friend-
ship*
162 Madison Avenue
New York, NY 10017
(tel. 212 679 4577)

Sovfracht USA Inc.
277 Park Avenue
New York, NY 10017
(tel. 212 355 6280)

Soviet Consulate General
2790 Green Street
San Francisco
California 94123
(tel. 415 922 6642)

US–USSR Trade and Economic Council
805 Third Avenue, Floor 14
New York, NY 10022
(tel. 212 644 4550)

Bank for Foreign Trade (Vneshtorgbank)		**Moscow**
Plushchikha 37	246 67 88	*bank*
Krasnopresnenskaya 12	253 17 99	

contacts

Actors' House
All-Russia Theatrical Society
Ul. Gorkovo 16   229 91 52
Architects' Union
Ul. Shchuseva 3   290 25 79
Art Workers' House
Pushechnaya 9   221 99 44

Artists' Union
Gogolevsky Bulv. 10   290 41 10
Composers' Union
Ul Nezhdanovoy 8/10   229 35 21
Film Makers' Union
Ul. Nezhdanovoy 8/10   250 41 14
Journalists' Union
Zubovsky Bulv. 4   201 77 70
Scientists' House
Kropotkinskaya 16   202 54 44
Teachers' House
Pushechnaya 4   221 52 67
Writers' Union
Ul. Vorovskovo 52   291 63 50

*House of Friendship with Peoples of
Foreign Countries*
Pr. Kalinina 16   290 20 69

Moscow Patriarchate
Chistiy per. 5   201 23 40
Muslim Organisations in the USSR
Foreign Dept.
Metrostroyevskaya 49   243 68 69
Soviet Peace Committee
Pr. Mira 36   280 33 82

*Ukrainian Friendship and Cultural
Relations Society*
Ul. Kirova 32, Kiev 21   93 01 67
USSR Chamber of Commerce and Industry
Ul. Kuybisheva 6   923 43 23
US–USSR Trade and Economic Council
Nab. Shevchenko 3   243 40 28

Moscow Central Customs House	*customs*
Komsomolskaya pl. 1	208 60 65
Road Freight Imports	
Butovo, 26km	
Varshavskoye Chaussee	541 76 21
International Post Office (inquiries)	
Varshavskoye Chaussee 37a	111 05 13

Phone inquiries	09	*directory*
Addresses	05	

Australia		*embassies*
Kropotkinsky per. 13	246 50 11–17	
Britain Nab. Morisa Toreza 14	231 85 11	
Commercial Office,		
Kutuzovsky 7/4	241 10 35	
Doctor	231 85 11	
Cultural Section	233 45 07	
Canada Starokonyushenny per. 23	241 91 55	
India Ul. Obukha 6-8	297 08 20	
New Zealand Ul. Vorovskovo 44	290 12 77	
United States		
Ul. Chaikovskovo 19/23	253 24 51–59	
Embassy club, commercial office,		
cultural section and doctor can be		
reached on these numbers		

Fire	01	*emergencies*
Militia (Police)	02	
Ambulance	03	
Gas	04	
Lost children	401 99 82	

Lenin Library (permission to export books)		*exporting*
Ul. Marksa/Engelsa 16		
(Monday and Friday 1 to 4 p.m.)	203 14 19	
Art Export Commission		
Ul. Chekhova 29		
(Tuesday 10 to 2 p.m.)	221 32 58	

health   *Diplomatic Polyclinic*
    home calls   237 39 04
    inquiries   237 83 38
    4th Dobryninsky per. 4   237 59 33

Tourists' Polyclinic (also looks after foreign
students and employees in
the USSR)   254 43 96
British Embassy doctor
Nab. Morisa Toreza 14   231 85 11

US Embassy Doctor
Ul. Chaikovskovo 19/23   253 24 51–59

ministries   *Ministry of Foreign Affairs*
    Smolenskaya Sennaya 32/34
    (inquiries)   244 16 06
    Press Department   244 41 12
Ministry of Foreign Trade
Smolenskaya Sennaya 32/34
(inquiries)   244 19 47
Ministry of Culture
Arbat 35, Foreign Department 248 08 04

registration   OVIR (visas and residence permits)
Kolpachny per. 10   924 93 49
Registration of accidents   02
Car registration
GAI Prospekt Mira 15   221 93 60
Number plates Podkopaevsky per. 4 297 93 87
Licences UPDK Kursovoy 1   202 40 83

service   UPDK (Diplomatic Corps Service *Bureau*)
    Kropotkinskaya 20 (inquiries) 201 23 26
    Booking at Zavidovo   201 27 17
    General Service Dept. Kursovoy 1 202 26 93
    UPDK Workshop, Kievskaya 8 240 20 92
Autoservice Station No 7
Selskokhozyaistvenny
Proyezd 6   181 06 31/181 13 74

Autoservice Centre,
Gorbunovskaya 14   448 42 68
   Volvos only, Entrance 5   448 80 35
Breakdown Service, Varshavskoye
Chaussee 87   119 80 00/119 81 08
Radio and TV repairs
Krutitsky Val 3, K. 2   276 47 14/276 47 21

Ordering by phone   225 00 00/227 00 40   *Taxis*
For cargo   256 90 03

Central Telegraph Ul. Gorkovo 7   *telephone*
Cables by phone in the USSR   225 20 02   *and*
International Calls   8194/8196   *telegraph*
Long-distance calls in the USSR   07
(inquiries in English)   8194

Intourist (Head Office) Moskva K—9   *travel*
Prospekt Marksa 16   292 22 60
   Telex   7211—16
American Express
21A Sadovo-Kudrinskaya   254 44 95
   Telex   413075 SU
Aeroflot Ul Dobryninskaya 7   238 85 35
Morflot (Soviet shipping companies)
Kalinina 21   291 93 31
Soviet Railways (Intourist inquiries in English)
Hotel Metropol, Prospekt
Marksa 1/4   221 45 13
Barry Martin Travel (business trips)
Hotel Soyuz-2 Room 323,
1, Krasnogvardeisky Proyezd 256   256 7433
   Telex   411446
British Airways
Krasnopresenenskaya Nab. 12 Fl 19
Office 1905   253 24 82—84
   Telex   413197

Maps

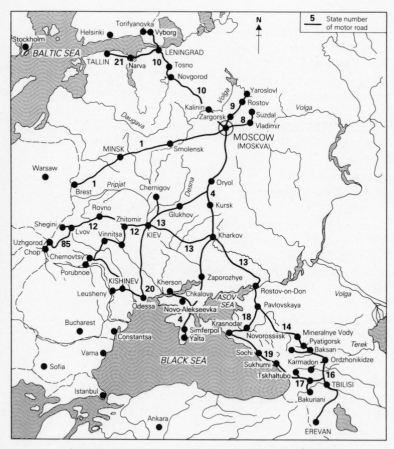

Principal cities and motor routes for visitors to the USSR

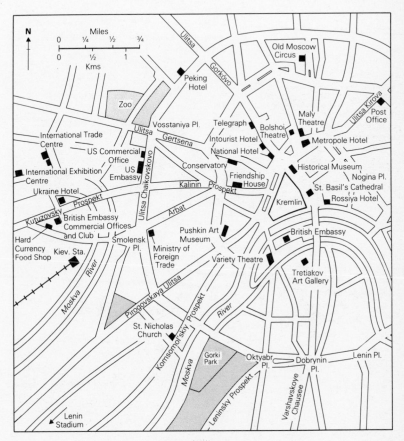

Central Moscow

METRO LINES

Interchange Station

The Moscow Metro

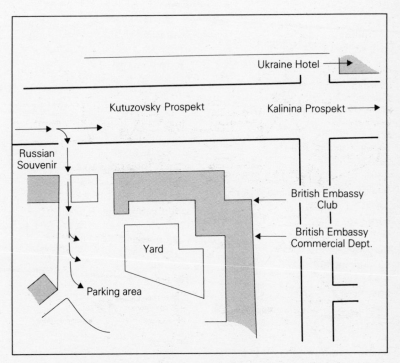

British embassy commercial offices and club, Moscow

Index

Suggestions

This page can be used to send in your suggestions for improving the book. What vital matters have been overlooked? What difficulties and pitfalls have been neglected or glossed over? What else should the intending visitor know about the quirks of the Russian way of life? Please write and tell us.

If your suggestions are adopted in any future edition, you will receive a free copy in recognition of your services in helping other people cope with Russia.

===

Please send your suggestions to Robert Daglish, c/o Basil Blackwell Ltd, 108 Cowley Road, Oxford OX4 1JF.

Name . . . .

Address . . . .

. . . .

My suggestions are